bombay
in the Age of Disco:
City, Community, Life

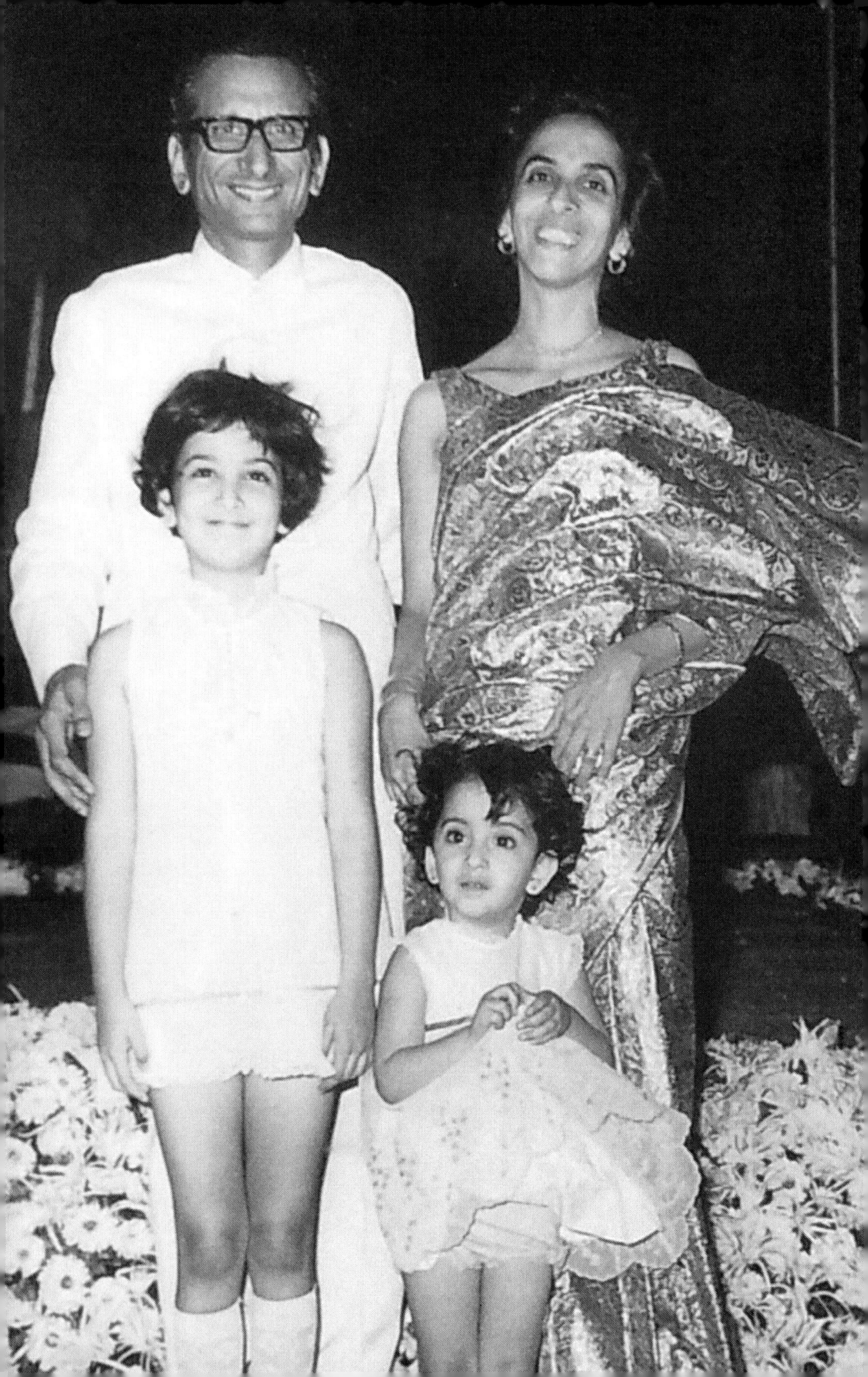

bombay
in the Age of Disco:
City, Community, Life

TINAZ PAVRI

Copyright © 2015 Tinaz Pavri

All rights reserved. No part of this book may be reproduced in whole or in part without written permission from the publishers, except by reviewers who may quote brief excerpts in connection with a review in newspaper, magazine, or electronic publications; nor may any part of this book be reproduced, stored in a retrieval system, or transmitted in any form or by any means electronic, mechanical, photocopying, recording, or other, without written permission from the publisher.

Some names, identifying details, and incidents or events have been changed. A few scenes have been modified or conflated or their time-frame changed to build the story. Ultimately, the author recognizes that others may remember events in this book differently from how they reside in her memories.

Published by:
University of North Georgia Press
Dahlonega, Georgia

Printing Support by:
BookLogix
Alpharetta, GA

Cover design by Corey Parson and Jon Mehlferber

Cover photograph courtesy of Arun Viswam

Frontispiece courtesy of the author

ISBN: 978-1-940771-17-5

Printed in the United States of America, 2015
For more information, please visit ung.edu/university-press
Or email ungpress@ung.edu

For my boys

Contents

Bombay/Mumbai 1
An Office in Flora Fountain 7
Saturdays with Mamina 13
We Were Parsis 29
West Breeze, Sea Breeze 36
Sangeeta Building 48
Putli 57
School at Mahim Bay 63
Weekends at Khandala 71
Excellent Women 81
Bombay Birthdays 88
The Day Indira was Shot 98
Leaving Bombay 111
Glossary 117

Chapter 1

BOMBAY/MUMBAI

I didn't know it at the time of course, but the Bombay I left, my Bombay, city of all my dreams ever since, was in the last throes of its pre-globalized past. Although in the eighties we considered ourselves as urbane and sophisticated as real city-dwellers anywhere, there was still not a latte, or Frappuccino or McMaharaja—McDonald's first, much-anticipated Indian Big Mac—to be had. The ubiquitous global chains had not muscled their way into impossibly-priced prime real-estate, and dirty, crumpled five-hundred-rupee notes were not falling out of the latest monstrous Louis Vuitton canvas bags like monopoly money. The city was really Bombay, even in name, when I left, a warmer, shyer, slower self that, at the time, we still felt had steadily deteriorated over the years from something even more precious and fast-fading, slipping from our fingers and memories even as we lived in its buildings and walked its pot-holed roads and boarded its overflowing trains and buses and gazed at its sea-line, breathing in its moist, slightly fetid air, and dreaming about being somewhere else.

When I returned in 1995, it had become Mumbai, literally. As if the name-change had also waved a wand, a tenser, more divided, more modern, and chaotic new city was emerging. Television now had hundreds of channels and was de rigeur in households both skyscraper and slum. The unmistakable signs of globalization were springing up all over the city, wherever room could be carved for them and even where it could not, for there was no longer space for anything with the city's population skyrocketing and new entrants claiming their Bombay dream daily. New slick or shoddy malls even had underground car-parks of sorts (albeit, flooded with the first onset of the monsoons in true Bombay fashion) where makeshift valets in tattered uniforms ran up to park your car, now more likely to be a flashy new top-of-the-line global model than an ancient Fiat or Ambassador, those lumbering old boats sputtering down our childhood roads and gullies, spewing carbon and stench. There were now

Cineplexes, multiplexes, and even bowling allies where globally-savvier kids were the new Mumbaikars, leaving us Bombayites of yore to eat their dust. Even foreign—"phoren"—Bombayites, the vaunted abroad-returned, who were used to being welcomed back each year with equal measures of envy, obsequiousness, and affection, were no longer the objects of the new Mumbaikars' desires. After all, they were too busy with their new access to goods, places, and jobs that companies from all over the world were creating at breakneck speed; or they were too crushed by the hard new city to care about the returnees from once-coveted countries in the West whose economies were now fading and sputtering and showing feet of clay. Questions about America, though still asked, were not as laced with longing: Mumbai itself had become American—and European, Asian, African. Mumbai was now a global city and the world was in it.

I didn't know when I left that mine was the last generation of true Bombayites, literally and figuratively. Our generation had straddled the last decade of Nehruvian socialism, longed for "abroad" so that we could be a part of the "real" world–concerts, theatre, cultural life, global connectedness, and even the more mundane things—globally-branded clothes, shoes, makeup, underwear—that the mixed-model Indian economy had denied us our whole lives, and we had tolerated everything. We had created our own little Londons and New Yorks in our Bombay apartments, had eaten not in chains but at beloved old cafés that were built by the longings and imaginings of real Bombayites creating their image of the world, that few in reality had actually seen, in our own city. We hung out at the Max Mueller Bhavan, British Council, the Jehangir Art Gallery for what seemed at the time lavishly-sponsored global, intellectual life that held the whiff of freedom, daring, and questioning of taboos or, closer to home, at Prithvi Theatre which continually presented abstruse plays like *Rosencrantz and Guildenstern are Dead* that we never admitted being confounded by. We jostled in packed trains to colleges in "town," South Bombay, the best (and possibly only) alternative for those hungry for a life beyond the parameters of our everyday city, so wide and varied, but for us growing up, still so confining! South Bombay with its air of worldly sophistication and graceful, grand-shabby historic and pre-independence architecture allowed us to dream bigger, of other coveted places and other possible lives, even while Bollywood dreams were being furiously created in the North Bombay suburbs for other Bombayites who desired them. Our Bombay easily accommodated both—after all, it was not known as The City of Dreams for nothing.

Now the center of the city has shifted to wherever money dictates. Flashy new shops and restaurants have made the friendly, laid-back Bandra and sleepy-sultry Juhu shining Meccas in the new Mumbai, with steel and glass skyscrapers towering over the remaining bungalows and low-rises. Rapacious builders have offered unimaginable sums of money, and sometimes failed to pay it, to raze older art-deco bungalows and cram yet another multi-storied building in amid the debris. Other Meccas that I have never seen, complete with mega-malls in far-flung Malad and Kalyan, claim their stake in the city. South Bombay is a little startled at its slackening grip over the pulse of the new city, taken aback, but too grand and too old to be unduly bothered by the new upstarts yet.

In a coincidence, the city's name was returned to its supposedly pre-colonial moniker Mumbai, by a chauvinist Maharashtra state government who used a misguided nationalism to further its own divisive political agenda, at around the same time the country's economy was transformed. The Congress party, led by P.V. Narasimha Rao, took the first steps towards serious integration with the world economy in the early nineties from India's hitherto mixed-economy/quasi-socialist, post-colonial model favored by its first Prime Minister Jawaharlal Nehru. Bombay, then, will always be the pre-global child, bearing the last vestiges of Nehru's dream of economic self-sufficiency through trade restrictions and import substitution, which, even when I lived there, had deteriorated to something much less for many, finding its place in a world which had still not been transformed by the rapid and insistent thrust of a seductive and rapacious trans-nationalization, where the inanity of the twitterati had not lowered the discourse, where yearning was still possible. Mumbai is different. Mumbai is brash. Mumbai is bold, fast, divided, hard, and less inclined to look around itself at beloved buildings and landmarks and smile, shudder, or sigh with the hope and hopelessness of a love that, despite all odds, binds one forever to this city of one's childhood foibles and growing-up angst.

After two decades in the U.S., just when I thought I had lost Bombay forever to Mumbai, the city was hit with the terrorist attacks of November 26, 2011—26/11, as they became referred to across the country—India's own 9/11. The images of the wildly burning Taj hotel, a scene of childhood wonder at its singular, gentle grandeur, seemed to underline the physical passing of that terror-free city of my childhood. Blood and chaos reigned in the lugubriously gothic Victoria Terminus that spewed hundreds of thousands of people every hour onto its platforms, minutes from the forbidding stone façade of St. Xavier's college where I had spent five transformative years.

In the days that followed, on blogospheres and airspaces that I accessed from my far-away city in America, I heard refrains of anger and sorrow about my poor bloodied city that might have been my very own. I realized that not only was I not alone, with millions of Mumbaikars all over the world and Bombayites—my Bombayites—churning with the same feelings, but that I would, because of this city, never be alone. Because if Bombay was burnt in my memory forever, it was also etched in the minds of these others: friends from school, rivals at college, neighbors in the buildings next to mine leaning out of their balconies and staring unblinkingly for "time-pass" (oh, that uniquely Indian activity of whiling away the hours!) at people and traffic outside, fellow travelers on the Bombay locals, taxi riders, rude bus conductors, and office-goers marching out of step on crowded, chaotic streets, trying to make their lives in this difficult, beloved city; and still others, who like I, watched and visited and loved the city from afar. They—we—still believed. As the fires were brought under control on my 24/7 computer screen with the mournful/panicked NDTV background music imprinted in my brain, and as my frantic phone calls were answered a million miles away by breathless, shocked, familiar voices, I understood that this venerable old city, this grande dame of my memories, could not be brought to its knees easily.

In the tumult grew a need to write what I remembered. My city, my childhood, my Bombay. We were a generation not made special by the end of an era as Rushdie's midnight's children might have been. We were not distinguished as the builders of a new India, as fledgling post-independence generations were in Nayantara Sahgal's *Rich Like Us*, nor pitied like the last of the Indo-Europeans left behind and slipping into irrelevance in Anita Desai's *Baumgartner's Bombay*. But we are keepers of the memory of a different Bombay, a city that stood at the edge of tremendous transformation to come, but that moment, that time, those decades and years stood still and embraced us. And for me, another need—to express the pain of inexorably losing, literally and physically, the Parsi community which surrounded me in its rambunctious and warm embrace and put its indelible imprint on my life as one of only a very few in a city of many, many millions, just as it had put its imprint on Bombay itself over hundreds of years.

A city is necessarily experienced differently and singularly by each of those who live in its thrall. For many in Bombay, this embrace is cold and hard, a vice whose tentacles encircle and squeeze, knocking down your huts and razing your slums, kicking you and leaving you for dead in its streets for others to step over with the sad skill of practice. For others, the luckier ones, the embrace is warmer. You strive and struggle and escape the squalor and emerge in a sweeter light. You live another day to dream in the City of Dreams. Bombay is full of stories of those who rose from the slums, from abject poverty, from nothing, to "make it" in the city that allowed for this class transformation to happen.

Or, luckiest yet, you are born in the gentle shadows of a home built almost a century ago by your grandfather, when the British were still playing out their final act in India. Yours is a flat that is sturdy and expansive, and offers the space to be filled with the love and laughter of endless relatives and friends, and with the bittersweet missteps of growing up. A home which, during Grandpappa's time, had the Arabian Sea as its frontispiece as it looked clear out to Juhu Beach's lapping, surf-tipped waves, but that today is crowded in by tall new skyscrapers on all sides, pushing at its generous curves and lines, creating dark shadows within, gloomily trapping the twilight of the past—of lost family, lost community, and lost city. I know that the sights and sounds, the neighborhoods, buildings, and streets that I grew to love were inaccessible to millions who left their huts to labor outside only to return to squalor at dusk. But I believe that they had their own Bombay dream, as each of us did. This huge, filthy, maddening, beautiful city gave us all the space to think big, to love tenaciously, to live and dream within its crowded veins and arteries.

It also gave us something else: an abiding love of city. When you grow up in a city, and if that city is throbbing, gritty, hardworking, and real, not a plastic, highway-dependent excuse for suburbia-disguised-as-city, you are instantly at home in so many other cities of the world. And when you grow up as part of a tiny, urban minority in a city which, incredibly and improbably, your own community stamped with a most powerful and outsize imprint, the city—a city—is a fundamental part of who you are and what you know. Powerful nostalgia grips you in the most unlikely of places: in well-heeled or downtrodden London streets where the red double-decker buses remind you of the dusty old carbon-spewing BEST buses careening through Bombay streets with arms and legs hanging out of their open doors and smirking conductors officiously preventing your entry with suppressed glee. Regarding Bombay's ubiquitous BEST buses—BEST standing for Bombay Electric Supply and Transport—I must report that endless jokes were made at their expense. "Best buses, best, best?" friends and relatives would query. "You mean worst, the worst!" This mirth and other more salacious acronyms in place of the actual one, made our rough and challenging journeys on these buses easier to bear.

Or longing for Bombay hits you in corner cafés of Amman, reminiscent of the disappearing Bombay-Irani restaurants. Or when you look up at long-windowed buildings on a tree-lined Paris arrondissement and see instead the stately flats overlooking with such an arrogant complacency the dusty green Oval Maidan below. Or even when you walk down the Boulevard des Anglais in Nice—*tadan*—Marine Drive, exactly like it. And of course in all of New York, which Bombayites claim and love as their own, even though it looks nothing like it—there is something about the day-and-night energy, the freedom to love it in the way you choose. And in Rome, where the squat golden-hued buildings and loud chaotic traffic are reminiscent of our own remaining low-rise apartment buildings set on narrow auto-unfriendly streets. And in Ankara, where a heaped-high dry-fruit store or a wafting scent from a street-vendor's kebab stall in the evening will feel comfortable, familiar, and like home. *Tadan* Bombay. "Just like home," becomes our refrain as we traipse around the world, trying to forget when we are young, and then to re-learn when we are older, only to find out in the end that we may have left this city but this city will never leave us. It exists, even in transformed guise, in the landmarks, buildings, and train stations, in the continuing open-mindedness and stoicism of its inhabitants, in the incredible knowledge of how such infrastructural chaos and punishing challenge can still somehow order and shelter the lives of so many, and most importantly, in the collective memories of us, its children—Bombay's children—who knew it then and remember it now.

Chapter 2

An Office in Flora Fountain

My enduring love affair with South Bombay, "town" as we called it, began with the trips to my maternal grandmother's home every Saturday while she was alive. On those mornings, as with other essential trips to town for movies, plays, visits to relatives and shopping, Paps (the moniker my younger sister, Rashna, and I gave to our father, Bomi) good-humoredly allowed us women—my mother, Rashna, and I—to ride with him. Daily he drove from home in Santacruz to his Flora Fountain office, where he presided over a modest staff of four. In the cramped quarters of a grand-crumbling colonial building in the Fort district where such centuries-old buildings rubbed shoulders with each other, the busiest old business district in town where the big deals were made, and old and reputed companies had their headquarters, Paps had quietly and unhurriedly built his own professional life of architect. This he had done without many of the resources or the requisite parental assistance common for those of his social class and certainly common for many Parsis of the time. The Pavris were not without resources—after all, Grandpappa had been a builder with some success, especially in the suburbs, having built residences for wealthy Parsis, including the billionaire Pallonji Mistry's father, Shapoorji, and of course our own compound in Santacruz holding the two buildings, West Breeze and Sea Breeze, that housed the families of Paps and all his siblings. At the height of his profession, Grandpappa had even built a residence (a palace of sorts) for the Maharajah of Jodhpur. Paps had told the story of how his parents, along with their tiny firstborn, Amy, had visited one of the Jodhpur palaces in the 1920s, the time before independence when the maharajahs ruled (India's princely states were autonomous and these kings "owned" their kingdoms then). Amy had been placed in a solid silver cradle to nap while my Grandmamma had engaged the Maharani in conversation! But Grandpappa's fortunes were waning as Paps began his professional life, and in any case, Paps was not one inclined to ask anyone, even family, for help.

Outside his office windows, we drank in the sights that underscored our wonder for South Bombay. We could see the statue of the Roman goddess of spring, Flora, built in 1864, perched on top of the sporadically functioning fountain. Not having lost her lonely beguiling charm, and even more miraculously not having broken or crumbled in the punishing twin combination of Bombay neglect and careless desecration, Flora has, for well over a century, created a small circle of tranquility around which traffic honks and screeches on the busy Dadabhai Naoroji Road. Centuries old neoclassical buildings, some crumbling themselves, look down with amiable indifference. We would see buildings that housed important-sounding banks—American Express, Mercantile, and the Bank of India—restaurants, cafés, shops, and people purposefully walking towards their business through rows of orderly road-side hawkers and second-hand book-sellers. Nearby was the Vatcha Agiary, the fire temple with two huge winged bulls carved in stone at the entrance in Assyrian/Persian-Zoroastrian style.

We seldom visited Paps' office because it was at the other end of town from our home in Santacruz, but whenever we did, we were thrilled at the evidence of his profession laid out in front of us. There were the drawing boards spread with blueprints of buildings and factories he was designing in far-flung suburbs like Vashi and Kandivali, most in a low-hung, angular, many-paned, Bombay-modified-modernist style of his hero Frank Lloyd Wright, whom some of his peers at the Sir Jamsetjee Jeejeebhoy (J.J.) School of Art had studied under.

Along with the compasses, square rules, drafting tables, and models, were the papers, pencils, and colored pens that had obviously come "from abroad," so smart did they look in their unfamiliar boxes and bags. In those days, ironically for a country which had created exquisite art, prose, and sculpture over millennia, anything of sophisticated function or finish (or sometimes, anything that simply *worked*) inevitably came "from abroad." It was *phoren* and coveted by those who could and could not afford alike. In the sixties, seventies, and into the eighties, India was still living out the mixed-economy model that Prime Minister Nehru put in place at the time of independence. While the economy had reached its stated aim in certain areas—some Indian industries like iron and steel or textiles, sheltered from foreign competition or nationalized over the decades, had indeed strengthened—in many other areas India fell far behind the competitive standard being set in other parts of the world for products, including in other Asian countries. The story goes that Indian politicians visiting Beijing and Shanghai in the eighties returned home in shock at just how far China had left India behind. In daily life, Indians took this uneven development in their stride, learned to know the difference between what was worth the extra cost for *phoren* and what would suffice in its Indian guise. Everyday consumer items like letter paper or t-shirts or ballpoint pens were all shoddy cousins of their sleekly-finished, *and functional,* Western and, increasingly, other Asian counterparts. We would marvel at the glossy aerogrammes that arrived from relatives in England—baby blue, beautifully lettered, *and* with sides that glued perfectly (oh my!)— unthinkable for our rough, blue paper airmail letters that crumpled and tore and whose sides had to be stuck down with the extra-strength glue using Fevicol's large and ungainly brush.

The substandard quality of many Indian consumer goods lingered for years after the economy's opening in the late eighties and early nineties, and is only now beginning to improve, in many cases significantly. In the last few years, I have been struck by the competent, confident finishes and well-articulated details on many things from birthday cards and toilet-paper to cars and other things that had remained painfully crude in the past (although of course, access to toilet paper or even toilets is out of reach for hundreds of millions still, as globalization widens the gap between those who have and those who still don't or could ever hope to). Standing now in my childhood friends' new apartments, where the interiors look like replicas of those in haute design magazines anywhere, I realize that those with money can now buy things to rival the most lavish anywhere in the world, even though slums seem to have spread further and cover ever wider swathes of the city. Spurred by global competition, the things money can buy have undeniably improved but few seem able to buy them, although it does appear that in some cases upward mobility is slowly, too slowly, becoming both possible and evident.

In a shift that mirrors the city's own recent metamorphosis, my father, the architect, painter, and aesthete who instilled in us a love for art as both function and form, continues to live in our childhood home where my sister, Rashna, and I notice increasingly crumbling plaster and cranky plumbing. In the new India, you see, everything has become very expensive. And, my mother and father, like many of their generation, move more slowly now and notice less the soft decay of the sturdy old home built by my grandfather before independence, as two separate buildings and encircled by a stout compound wall, for his five children who formed the Pavri clan. They mirror the slow downfall in the demography, fate, and fortunes of the Parsis themselves—still outlandishly prosperous by any average Indian standard—but certainly off from their pinnacles of achievement in centuries past and still a little dazed by their decline.

When we visited Paps' office, we sat at his drawing boards and tried our hands at sketching with secret flourishes while his many-talented (by necessity, because they had to juggle so many jobs) assistants hurried to bring soft drinks and sandwiches from the famous open-fronted street-level Irani restaurants close-by—Perkes, Parisian, Marosa. Much has been written about the loss of Bombay's Irani restaurants, those cafés built by Parsi and later-arriving Irani Zoroastrians, with their simple wooden chairs, wood-and-marble café tables, and menus of cakes, pastries, biscuits, meat, and chicken patties, and other savories that Bombayites rich and poor sat down to enjoy with hot cups of chai. Although the restaurants were fewer in my childhood than they had been during our parents' time, the decline has been precipitous and exponential in the new millennium. Few Irani-restaurateurs can afford the sky-rocketing rents on prime, street-fronted real-estate, and of those who own their spaces, few can resist offers to sell.

From these cafés, chicken sandwiches were (and still are) my eternal favorite. In between slices of thin, soft, buttered white bread, delicately shredded strands of chicken were placed, and mild English-Indian mustard added. These were considerably enhanced by being dipped in ketchup, I thought, and like many Indians who loved their tomato sauce, always ordered it on the side. It didn't matter what time we were visiting or whether we were hungry or not, because these were the rituals that had to be completed when we visited Paps's office in town.

As he and Mum sat and sipped coffee or tea, as the time dictated, I thought about a man growing up after the British had left, struggling to start a career on his own and choosing not to join larger firms that might have had more ambitious lives to offer. Had his dreams been fulfilled in the small office filled with easels and paintbrushes and blueprints and sketch-pens at the top of the wondrous-busy Fort Street? Or did it feel lonely or restrictive to sketch for his modest clients the small factories and warehouses done in his spare, mid-modernist style of which he *seemed* quietly satisfied, in a space where he was the single architect and the few others were draftsmen, assistants, and jacks-of-all-trades? We girls were immensely proud of Paps's designs, pointed out to us in Vashi, a "new Bombay" being built on the edges of the city, on our way to Khandala, or in Poona, where the industrialist Kirloskar had commissioned a retreat, a low-hung bungalow that melded into its lush green surrounds. Paps always waxed philosophical about life, but had he once wanted more: a bigger office, more staff, flashier things, taller buildings, more excitement, or to be "making lots of money," as Mummy constantly reminded him his friends, DM and Rama and Zal from the J.J. School of Arts, were indeed making by then?

Others of his cohort who were not interested in money like Nari Gandhi, were still gaining widespread recognition. As one of Bombay's finest architects in the 1960s, Gandhi was an ascetic, long-maned loner, who was a Frank Lloyd Wright disciple, and who people didn't know whether he was mad or a genius, as so often he was seen aimlessly walking bare-foot on Juhu beach. Staring into the horizon across the dirty waves, his clothes in tatters, his gaze benignly on the vista, Gandhi was celebrated for his integrity and brilliance; Paps, unsurprisingly, admired him most of all. But Paps's own talent was unheralded and his income modest. No Nari Gandhi and no DM, Paps's friend whose business had soared with big hotel projects and other buildings, Paps designed his buildings in the shadows of his more famous friends despite Mum's sometimes scarcely-concealed dissatisfaction that wrestled with her praise for his talent and independence. He lived then and since on his own terms and reaped, I hope, the rewards of his quiet integrity.

In Paps's office, surrounded by the excitement of the Fort area, we ate our sandwiches and drank our cold drinks as Mum and Paps drank their tea or coffee, brought up from the busy tea-shops below who made a cacophonous business supplying all the area offices with the essential beverage, sending young boys with precariously-balanced trays filled with glasses of hot chai at regular intervals. In Bombay, we were driven by a strict timetable for drinks and for meals, as for many other things. Tea was the ubiquitous morning beverage, but eleven o'clock was always coffee-time in my house. The preference was always for instant coffee with chicory, and only today is the concept of brewed coffee from beans catching on as international franchises have arrived, including Starbucks who ironically in a country that used to covet *phoren*, have been at pains to underline that they source their coffee only from India. In fact, one Starbucks, located a mere few steps from West Breeze-Sea Breeze, does such bustling business that cars clog the road as drivers drop off well-heeled customers who seem to have no problem paying several times the prevailing price for their lattes and cappuccinos. To me, however, the new brewed coffee never rivals the strong, bold flavor of the Nescafé or Bru that was drunk steaming hot with frothy milk and a bold helping of sugar.

Afternoon was always tea-time, but later in the evening, before the cocktails started, coffee could be had. And so Mum and Paps drank whatever the time dictated. To have done otherwise would have been to go against tradition, and my mother, Gool, would surely have remarked loudly to anyone within earshot, "Who drinks tea at eleven (or coffee at four)—what nonsense!" Indeed, poor Paps, that most faithful creature of habit, would sometimes finish his evening coffee extremely late and within an hour feel compelled to embark on his first whisky, for that's just what the hour dictated, and our housekeeper, Mary Lunjen, would have laid out the glasses and ice without fail and without reminder, at precisely eight thirty.

These interludes at Paps's office were never long, and we would leave him and move on to our town errands or visits or shopping or lunch at

Mamina's—my grandmother's. Or, if we had stopped in on the way home, we would all leave together for our long drive home. They were, and remain, small but sure stitches in our strong connection to the city, the layers of British and neoclassical architecture comfortably clothed in post-independence neglect, handsome, shabby, changing, harkening to the history of many centuries and the different peoples, Portuguese, Arab, Persian, Chinese, Jewish, from far-flung corners of the world, as well as myriad indigenous and Indian ethnic groups, sons and daughters of Maharashtra soil, who had called it home long before globalization became a noun.

Chapter 3

SATURDAYS WITH MAMINA

Most Saturdays, Paps would drop us three females off at Gowalia Tank, so named because on a small hill close by was a large water tank which had once functioned as a source for the area. Here Mamina, my grandma Coomie, had the ground floor flat of Khalakdina Terrace. Another leftover Anglicism, it was very common for Indian elite and middle-class alike to name their homes and buildings in echo of those in the English cities they had read about, and which the British had built in replica in Bombay and elsewhere in India, with the rather grand suffixes of Terrace or House or Hall, even if the homes themselves were modest. Of course, because Parsis were a uniquely successful minority in the fabric of Bombay's history, in Tardeo or Napean Sea Road or Colaba or Bandra but mainly in the Dadar Parsi Colony, you will see any number of such once-beautiful but now decaying bungalows and buildings.

We had ties to many of these homes in the Dadar Parsi colony. Thrity Terrace was where Coomie's family had lived over generations and is now, like all Bombay bungalows, under discussion for demolition and new-build. Dina Manzil, at the entrance of the colony, across from the colony's founder Mancherji Joshi's statue stands guard, was where Paps was born before Grandpappa shifted the family to Santacruz and built the Pavri compound there. There was Solipapa Cottage (whose sweetly eponymous name I loved—somebody's father or grandfather Soli!) and the four-terraced Palamkot Hall, my own Roda Aunty's house in the Colony, the home where my mother grew up. Mummy lived there with Roda, her mother's sister, because it was that much closer to her school in Mahim (the Bombay Scottish School, later to become my school as well) than Khalakdina Terrace in Gowalia Tank was. Also, Mamina had her hands full with Mum's sister, Mina, whose difficulties, peculiarities, and neuroses we never fully understood until much later, and who my own mother now tenderly takes care of, in place of her own mother, whose energies

Mina relentlessly once consumed (which the young Gool must surely have resented even if unconsciously).

The trips to Mamina's always started on a chaotic note. Paps waited patiently while we got our things together, things enough to last us for the rest of the day—books, changes of clothes, gifts, and offerings of food. For it was a "day-spend" we would be going for. A "day-spend"—at an aunty's, cousin's, or family friend's—would include a late morning arrival, a full (and most often very heavy and many-coursed) lunch to look forward to, a compulsory afternoon nap on actual or makeshift beds, cane-backed *chaises longues*, or sofas under softly-turning fans, followed by a sumptuous tea. We would stagger home in the evening, spent and talked-out, the four of us strangely alone again without the cacophony of extended family and friends. Rarely, a day-spend could stretch to include dinner. By then, the relatives would surely have exhausted all the gossip for the week or month and might have started a light bickering that would make us kids long even more to leave and return to our familiar neighborhood and friends whom we had had to leave behind for the day. But all was always well in the end. Kisses and hugs sent us off on our way, underlining the tight bonds of family reinforced over time until they were accepted, unquestioned, and unspoken—Indian style—and made lives all over our city infinitely richer. So many people to count on, turn to, accept without explanation, all a walk or drive or train ride away.

In the car going to Gowalia Tank for our day-spend, Rashna and I fought desultorily and insulted each other with a practiced ease while Mum and Paps turned a deaf ear. They spent their time chatting about relatives, friends, and how things had changed (in the old days this could never have been!), and the corruption, which even then had become the hallmark of Indian political life and today veritably paralyzes it, with one coalition government after another unable to forge a path through the morass. These kinds of things, I now know, are what parents everywhere say, as nostalgia for childhood always seems to make the past preferable to the present. Traffic was not light, but at least the car could keep moving as we wound our way down familiar roads in a way that is now impossible, taking as it sometimes does two hours to reach town from our north-western suburbs and indefinite and unpredictable amounts of time to go from anywhere to anywhere amid widespread infrastructural breakdown in the city today.

Leaving behind Bandra and Mahim, we passed Bombay Scottish on the left with the bay across from it and tried hard not to think about pending homework or how we would have to be back there on Monday. Paps navigated his way through Prabhadevi with the Siddhivinayak temple complex and milling worshipers on the left and then the open stretch of Worli and Mahalaxmi, where the sea suddenly reappeared. Roda Aunty's

Happy Home and School for the Blind, where she taught for so many years, stood on the left, the Hajiali mosque perched stoically amid the lashing waves as if it had been there forever, pilgrims seemingly treading a path through the waters, and South Bombay beckoned, more orderly and clean, with genteel pre-independence homes rubbing shoulders against new high-rises with glass-paned eyes that glittered in the sun and stared out onto the sea.

Invariably, Mummy would lament the loss of older homes that had made way for newer towers. "*Arre*, look at this ugly monstrosity they have constructed! Over here used to be my friend Dinaz's bungalow! How many times we used to go there for lunch! Now God knows where she is—probably migrated to England," as so many Parsis had—and to America, Australia, Europe, shrinking our small community further and further, leaving parents to grow old alone. Of course, those earlier post-independence buildings, a mix of mid-century European and soulless Soviet architecture are now shadows of the glitzier, glass-and-glamour skyscrapers that are defiantly shooting out of low-rise Bombay's (and particularly the Bandra-Khar-Santacruz suburbs') post-globalization landscape and could really be anywhere—Shanghai or Jakarta or Dubai—if one failed to look up and down at the road and see the carelessly-strewn garbage and variously-sized piles of fly-attracting excrement in front of their posh exteriors.

I loved the glamour of South Bombay. I loved its expansiveness, its slightly foreign look (to my suburban eyes), the sense of purpose and air of open cosmopolitanism and certainty that I felt the suburbs lacked (even though serious business was, of course, conducted there and although, on second thought, Bandra was nothing if not cosmopolitan). In South Bombay, I could forget that I was in Bombay at all and turn a dreamy eye to the green Hanging Gardens and Doongerwadi (the Parsi/Zoroastrian Towers of Silence) on the right, possibly the only real large patches of verdant green foliage and tropical exuberance left in the city, or the exclusive Kemp's Corner shops with zippy names like Vama and their unmistakably rich silks and leathers hanging insouciantly in large shining windows, and believe for a moment that I was somewhere else—Europe or America or Singapore or anywhere other than in Bombay.

Rashna always squealed when we passed Sterling Apartments on Pedder road before rounding Kemp's Corner and proceeding to Hughes Road, "Oooh! Sterling! My friend's cousin lives there and says it's the most prestigious building in Bombay!" And I, disparaging: "What rubbish! It's okay, nothing great." Because Rashna's friends could never be given such singular honors and my little sister was always to be put in her place.

Then the car would turn left from Hughes Road, passing the Gowalia Tank Maidan (now August Kranti Maidan) on the right, where I am told by my mother many a noisy independence rally was held in the early forties to which Mamina, my grandfather, and the family got front row seats from their *maidan*-facing, ground floor balconies (feeling *what* about the huge and inevitable transformations to come: exhilaration? trepidation? fear? pride?), and where Mahatma Gandhi gave his famous Quit India speech in 1942. Behind us on Hughes Road, we had just left Kharegat Colony with its wide, open balconies where old Parsis slowly hung out their clothes to dry or sat in their cotton *sudras* with cups of tea and impassively viewed the constant but, compared to the suburbs, sedate traffic. Sputtering, we would pull up outside the ground-floor flat of the massive block of Khalakdina Terrace. Urban European-style, it rose straight up from the road and footpath without benefit of a ubiquitous surrounding compound wall, and at the open front door Mamina would be waiting.

Eventually those Bombay vistas became embossed in my mind like the lushly embroidered flowers and birds and landscapes studding my aunties' beautiful silk *gara* saris. Once we passed the Bandra mosque with rows of skull-cap-wearing little children filing into the madrassah, I knew that our "area," the roving romping grounds that we were familiar with—with stretches of art deco Santacruz, leafy lanes of Khar with their hundred-year-old banyan trees incredibly left untouched still and bending graciously ever-closer to us and shrouding the *bania* shops and small clothing boutiques run by middle-class matrons in heavenly shade amid the scorching sun, the bungalow, and bakery-strewn Bandra—was now over. We were approaching Mahim with its glimpses of fishing-village-turned-slum, smell of rotting fish, and grey, rough sea on the right and rows and rows of depressing, ugly dilapidated government housing on the left.

Incredibly, even while new buildings rise on the ashes of old bungalows everywhere in the new Mumbai, these ghastly government-owned blocks, visible anywhere and everywhere in the city including in the most rarified parts of Bandra or Worli or Colaba, have remained untouched, soulless eyesores that are a testament to the unending failure of both civic responsibility and governmental accountability in India, underlining in equal measure the government's lack of imagination and surrender to corruption.

This is how Bombay stretched from north to south with the Arabian Sea a constant companion on its western side. This sea-lapped route was the one I knew best, whether it be in the suburbs or in town; the eastern half was mostly unknown to us, another of many Bombays. It was comprised of a tangle of railway stations on the eastern-railway side which would eventually end in VT (Victoria Terminus, one scene of the multiple 26/11 horrors), and endless chawls, those grim colonies of one or two room flats that were connected with long slivers of shared open balcony whose occupants' lives we couldn't bear to imagine, and yet understanding that they must have been infinitely better off than those existing in the slums, which in turn, with their "ownership" huts would have bested the hapless pavement dwellers and the utterly, completely homeless and destitute. So little did we see the visage of this side of Bombay and so seldom did we ask about it in those days, it could have been another city, with its mechanic shops, and bazaars, and pinched faces that told stories of hardship and want, and its juxtaposition even then of Bombay the beautiful against Bombay the cruel.

In our north-south journey, after leaving the triangular peaks of grey-clad Bombay Scottish staring into the sea, which absurdly always left a lump in my throat ("There stands our school on Mahim Bay!" opened our school song), we would make our way through Shivaji Park, stolid middle-class neighborhoods interspersed with squares of green gathering spaces, little parks and mini-*maidans*, unimaginable luxuries in space-starved Bombay and yet whose traditional and somewhat repressive air gave me a little pause. In Shivaji Park lived good, serious citizens unenlivened by Bandra-style frippery and, as in some other parts of Bombay I felt I would have stood out like a sore thumb, though never in beloved Bandra-Khar-Santacruz and never in town. Recently I've noticed open-air cafés and the semblance of a gayer, freer life in this and other suburbs that are asserting and reshaping their own identities in the new Mumbai.

Pedder Road was where we parted ways with the sea, our constant right-hand companion on the trip. The Arabian Sea is so important in establishing Bombay's identity and feel, its open expanses always allowing rich and poor to feel connected with the rest of the world and to imagine strange and glorious and attainable vistas across its horizon. Indeed you will see daily walking on its shores multitudes of slum children, poor and middle-class Bombayites, for whom this freeing outing by the sea costs nothing and is their equal right. To us children, these vast, constant waters served as inspiration, an igniter of imagination and longing like a good orchestra tuning up before a concert and making a big and strange and wonderful sound that promises all possibilities to come. If we had instead taken the right hand turn to Breach Candy, (where the Parsi General Hospital with its quiet green grottos and gardens and marble-tiled, antique-filled foyer had held my grandmother Coomie in her last days, as it would later hold my beloved Roda Aunty) we would have followed the sea's grey path into town for a little longer, winding up towards Walkeshwar and Malabar Hill and Paps's friend DM's and his wife, Uschi's apartment overlooking Chopatti beach and the asphalt stretch of the Queen's Necklace, but that was for another day.

Breach Candy, Napeansea Road, Pedder Road—thrilling, orderly neighborhoods filled with people who I was convinced led highly privileged lives and could shop at will at boutiques devoted to fine chocolates and gourmet groceries and branded clothes "from abroad" ("You can get ham and sausages straight from Germany at Amarsons and real Levi's at Premsons," my friends would assert with astonishment). On the way to Mamina's on Pedder Road, we would pass Jindal House, an industrialist's abode which consisted of a massive three story colonial home kept in pristine white, a near-impossibility in pollution-choked Bombay where most buildings wore a constant grey cloak of soot and mold, and surely allowing for a life within that was as foreign as living in the White House would be for most Indians. Riding over the Kemp's Corner Bridge I could peer into the windows of ancient, brown-faded low-rises, British-built with unexpected, grinning gargoyles or curlicues almost unrecognizable in their encrusted grime and surrounding gentle rubble. The bridge had been built with little thought or planning, as most things were in post-independence Bombay, within inches of these buildings' once-graceful facades. If the inhabitants straying onto their balconies and looking into our passing cars had stretched out their arms, and I mine, we might have touched fingertips.

In one of these once-grand buildings, Maskati House, in the curve of Kemps Corner, lived Rashna's Elphinstone College friends, two plump, dimpled Parsi sisters who loved to eat and loved opera and always blasted lament-ridden Puccini arias through the open windows of the decaying yellow building which had once been a beautiful, rounded-front, three-story, art nouveau structure. I think now of their lives, growing old together, the windows of marriage and family closing quickly for Parsis because of demographic realities or their own choices, joining the large and wonderful phalanx of spinsters and aunties like our Roda. They would no doubt hold implausible hen-parties, of the description Roda often provided, where they would play their arias until the old birds grew frailer and fewer, and the parties receded into a cherished past, to be re-lived with bewilderment in the changing city on a quiet day.

The Cadbury house, purple in reminiscence of the unforgettable chocolate covers themselves, stood out as a beacon of then-rare, fat, multinational corporate wealth among less showy buildings, and Rashna and I fantasized over the heaps of Fruit and Nut bars that it must surely have stashed in it somewhere. And on the right, the acres and acres of green, leafy Doongerwadi, where, according to our ancient Zoroastrian customs, our dead were taken, their bodies to be prayed over and left in their final open resting place for vultures to pick clean. Such gory goings-on could hardly be imagined when we looked at the dense foliage that continued for miles and contained exotic flora and fauna, and was surely the only place in Bombay where bright green peacocks strutted, besides of course Victoria Gardens, our decrepit, dispirited zoo, which even to my delighted childhood eyes appeared tired and shabby but may well have held a dejected peacock or two.

Inhabitants of the adjacent high-rises, however, were not so accommodating, and reported a certain queasiness in seeing the big birds hovering over the centuries-old gardens and, rumor had it, depositing the stray piece of flesh which could have been the appendage of an aunty or uncle on near-by rooftops and balconies. In recent times, the vultures have become nearly nonexistent in the city, and new ways of disposing of our dead are being debated among the Parsis, including burial and cremation. As children, we hardly paused to reflect on grandmas and grandpas over the centuries being plucked clean by vultures, as I sometimes now do. My own children recoil in horror as I tell them calmly that a dead body is a dead body and that I would not mind such an end at all. But alas, the vultures are now all gone and the efforts of certain community madmen (leaders) to "cultivate" and breed them anew in the city so that old traditions would be maintained against all odds (and sense) have thankfully come to naught so far.

All along our north-south route, billboards jostled with each other for space, many advertising the endless Bollywood films in all their drama, gore, and tears, manly studs and ravishing belles embracing atop buildings and bridges, creating an air of merriment and revulsion and drama all across the city. I remember the Amul Butter hoardings, clever weekly takes on topical issues, gently skewering politician and common man alike with their sly English-Hindi twist on words. And the tag-line, always "utterly, butterly Amul" with the cartoon Amul babies big-bellied and sated on the yellow, rectangular pats of butter. These hoardings Paps always remarked on with approval. "*Joyu, joyu*, did you see the new one? *Ketlu majhenu karech*, such a good job they do!" And Mum would nod vigorously, glad to agree. To be facile and clever with words and language was of supreme importance for this lover of Shakespeare, who could also at will recite (and butcher) Keats and Wordsworth, which to her consternation, were not taught at Bombay Scottish in any seriousness anymore, and therefore kept her girls in woeful ignorance. When we cheekily put it to Mum that her love of Shakespeare was the result of a colonized mind, she gave us a withering look and said if we believed that, then we were truly more foolish than she had thought and that Bombay Scottish was surely failing us. Regarding Amul, I see that it has not lost its clever touch: a 2011 Christmas-time ad ran, "Merry X'maska and a Snacky New Year!" You know, *maska*—butter. And in response to the gone-viral global ALS ice-bucket challenge in 2014, Amul had this rejoinder: an Amul baby holding aloft a bucket filled with pats of butter, exclaiming, "Slice butter-it challenge!"

And finally, after the long sweltering ride, Mamina! Mamina, standing spare and tall, grey hair immaculately waved, her sari and long-sleeved blouse always elegant, composed in a way that my mother never could be—bits and pieces of Mummy were always awry and falling about. After the death of her husband, a prominent Bombay lawyer who succumbed to a heart attack the year I was born, Coomie had lived life on her own terms, in a mostly non-rancorous standoff with her daughter-in-law while doting on her son and grandson, all together, joint-family style, as tradition dictated. She presided over a small army of servants including a well-trained cook and a driver who knew all the best routes to Marine Drive for our Saturday evening walks. Her slightly stern demeanor meant that I was always a little in awe of her, but I loved her strength and the way she always seemed in control of everything in a country where women (and sometimes even liberated Parsi women) had little control. Mamina stood up for herself, never backed down, and calmly put people in their place. Gool inherited her strength, but certainly not her calmness, for Mum could be rash and intemperate and rush in where Mamina would have chosen a withering look or simply silence. Because she held an uncanny resemblance to Indira Gandhi, I later grew a soft spot for Indira and almost forgave her unforgivable excesses; just as because of my Kobad uncle's rotund resemblance to Oliver Hardy, I cried foolishly in childhood movie theaters when he was bested by the sly and wily Laurel and his pants tore into shreds or he fell down precariously-pitched ladders and his lunch spilled in all directions and all the movie theatre howled in laughter except myself, who foolishly sniveled through it all.

Lunch at Mamina's was perfectly-orchestrated—main dish, side dish, gleaming silver cutlery (later to tarnish and blacken under Mummy's care and be lost, forgotten, stolen, or carelessly thrown away) in the right places. Mutton "pancakes," savory minced mutton enrobed in the softest of crepes, were my favorite, and Mamina never tired of sneaking those on the menu for me. Dessert (pudding) always followed. I remember Roda Aunty, who delighted in her food, asking her sister with interest, and before the meal was quite over, "Pudding *ma su che?* (What's for dessert?)" We kids would titter and correct, "But how can it be *pudding* when it's actually *ice cream*, Rodi?!" I only learned later that what I thought was yet another Parsi eccentric-ism was actually also, for their generation, the English way to refer to dessert, all dessert.

When we retired to Mamina's room for our post-lunch "afternoon sleep" (we were free to read instead, and Rashna and I often did, so bringing a sufficient quota of books that all kids devoured—Enid Blyton, Agatha Christie, Asterix, P. G. Wodehouse, Archie and Amar Chitra Katha comics, Nancy Drew—was imperative), I asked her to open the polished leather and wood jewelry boxes that stood on her Art Deco dressing table with its perfectly trifold wings holding the mirror in three parts. Some of these boxes had sepia-brown photos imprinted on them of fading and rather sinister-looking ancestors, females in traditional Parsi saris with their right-shouldered, richly-embroidered *pallus,* or males with tall, glossy black *fetas* crowning their heads (semblances of these hats I later saw in ancient images of Armenian gentlemen in the Hellenistic world of Cleopatra VII, underlining again our shared history in that part of the world). I never tired of looking through the beautiful old jewelry that was one hallmark of all Parsi families.

Once, I played with a heavy gold locket with a diagonally-set band of small emeralds and diamonds, enthralled by the fact that it could hold two small photos within and fantasizing about the photos I would place in it if it became mine. Perhaps there would be a photo of that infuriating boy in my class, Akash, whom I timidly and furtively watched from my seat in class, or maybe Roger Moore/James Bond with whom all Indian girls were in love at the time, Hollywood movies coming to Bombay theaters years later than their western releases. Mamina gave me the locket that day, which I excitedly took home, and proceeded clumsily and immediately to break the paper-thin glass within which the photos would be encased. Of course, Mummy slapped me soundly across one cheek ("a nice tight slap," as all Indian parents were fond of threatening their kids with). "Silly girl!" I deserved it. Years later, I saw the same heavy lockets in nineteenth century portraits of dowagers at the Portrait Gallery in Washington, D.C. Mamina's locket had apparently been all the rage in the late 1800s.

On other days she gave me other things: one dangling two-dropped emerald earring set in burnished gold, because in the olden days, she explained patiently, traditional Parsi women might cover their heads with the *pallu* of their saris and only have one ear exposed where they held out the open end of the *pallu.* To me these familial jewels—ruby and diamond brooches, geometrically-set diamond and emerald rings, tubular rope necklaces of dull Georgian gold, sets of ruby and diamond necklaces and earrings, and pearls, always the Parsi pearls, big, small, seed, rice, Basrai, all exquisitely crafted in Victorian or Art Deco settings like my gold horseshoe ring (for good luck), set with tiny Basra pearls given to me on my *navjote*, or my severely hexagonal diamond and emerald baguettes ring given on a birthday—came to represent a life beyond my imagining, a life that Parsis had lived for hundreds of years in their adopted country and city, sumptuous lives of now-impossible splendor, and filled me with the familiar sense of loss and longing for another era, another place, not necessarily the past, but somewhere where I wouldn't feel constantly and always an onlooker, gazing at what was supposed to be my life and seeing instead the remains of other lives, the ones before.

In South Bombay, Parsis were well represented in the villas, bungalows, and buildings that were invariably old, solid, and substantial. At Khalakdina Terrace, itself a hugely solid block of flats that spanned a large part of the street, Mamina's ground floor flat was enormous. Cavernous rooms with twenty-five-foot ceilings of the likes that I had not seen in any other Bombay flat except at Palamkot Hall, made one instantly feel a bit off balance, like a Lilliputian. An enormous drawing and dining room and three big bedrooms were situated unimaginatively off a long broad corridor, each with its own stretch of internal windows with wooden shutters looking out onto the corridor and thence to the street and the *maidan* beyond, around which a disorderly, hapless row of slums had sprung and whose raucous and pitiful footpath lives I watched in shamed fascination. In that corridor, Firi and I played cricket with our cousin Kayzad, who was an only child, adored and spoiled by his mother. It was a testament to Kayzad's good sense that he didn't allow the coddling, and in fact actively worked to sabotage it at every turn.

These rooms my architect father, with uncharacteristic acerbity, labeled "*tabelas*" or stables because low-hung false ceilings were all the rage then, and he had even attempted to have one installed in our own Santacruz living room with its still-high but more modest ceiling height before being shot down, expectedly, by Mummy. Then, he assumed a long-suffering air and mused that he had given up, that our mother never wanted any *improvement* of the home and, unconsciously waxing Socratic, that improvement—at all levels—was paramount for a well-lived life and not, as she scoffed, a "waste of time and money."

At four on Saturday evenings, the doorbell at Khalakdina Terrace chimed as if by clockwork and in was ushered Homi Uncle's stenographer, who had come for Dictation. With his stenographer's help, Homi Uncle caught up on an over-burdened week at work, barking out in his loud nasally voice (Paps called it the Rustom bray, and it was indeed and unfortunately shared by Roda and others of the clan, which means it actually came from Mamina's side, but Rustom bray seemed a fitting appellation) strangely stilted sentences like "herewith the defendant to incur penalties" and lovely terms like "testatrix" and "plaintiff." We giggled as a hapless legal saga, usually surrounding a disputed flat or property in a prime Bombay locale, unfolded for a Ms. Ruby Mistry or Messrs. Fali and Sorab Daruwalla. But amidst the fun I developed a keen ear for the music of legal language and enough interest in the law, with its clarity, precision, and adherence to order, that I wanted to pursue it in college. But later, since no U.S. law school would pay my way and my love of an imagined America trumped my love of the law, I settled on a Political Science doctorate, obligingly paid for by the American university to which I eventually would go.

Homi had taken on the practice of my grandfather and had become one of the most sought-after advocates in the city for property matters. In Bombay, with its limited space and unlimited demand for it, property was gold. Small, poky flats that we could never imagine living in were sold for untold *lakhs* and *lakhs* (now *crores* and *crores*) of *rupees.* Stories unfolded around people muscling their way into the houses and hearts of old Parsis with no "issues" (as Indians euphemistically labeled childlessness) and never leaving, the better to stake a claim on the flats after their deaths. I always puzzled over how it was that they *never* left—not even to go shopping or to the *bania* shop, or out for an airing, for work, for a walk—in a city where it seemed all of humanity was always outside? It was all very puzzling, but if they had left the flat, the true owner or heir or landlord could quickly place a *talla*, a big serious lock, on the entrance door and they might never get the chance to get back in! And in those days before fast-track courts, a property case in the courts could take thirty years or more to resolve, and often possession *was* the law. All of four feet something, my uncle became known as "the little lawyer" and soon the enormous, rich, brown mahogany dining table with its menacing claw feet was buried under the mounds of his rectangular legal briefs in their maroon and brown covers that dealt with these precise issues. Who had taken over the flat and from whom was of supreme importance and must be decided once and for all!

More than my uncle's legal prowess, Kayzad, Rashna, and I were enamored of the stenographer's rapid dots and dashes as he more than ably kept up with Homi's rapid pace and emerged fitfully to take full breaths. "Get him another cup of tea," my uncle's nasal tones barked to the cook, who hurried out with a fresh cup. "Okay, ready?" and he would launch relentlessly on to yet another case. I have no idea what would happen with this dictation—I suppose it was later typed up for my uncle to peruse in his office what he had extemporaneously and effortlessly dictated to his stenographer. Two or three hours later, the stenographer, whom we unceremoniously referred to as stenographer-uncle, would sheepishly and hurriedly gather his meager things and take his leave, recognizing his precarious position. Though he was certainly not a servant (for with his professional abilities he was indispensable to my uncle), even though Parsi, he was not quite of our class in the firmly-drawn social hierarchy of my childhood Bombay. And so he must not over-stay his welcome and he must hurry out as the shadows lengthened and Nilufer Aunty fretted and fidgeted about getting dressed late for "going out" and evening loomed.

Later in the new Mumbai, my friend heard from his friend that Homi Uncle was reputed to be not just one of the best advocates in Bombay, but also one of the most independent-minded. In a court system choked with corrupt officials, from underlings to lawyers to judges, and where justice was nothing if not arbitrary and for sale, my uncle didn't play dirty. In following the straight and narrow, I have no doubt that he passed up opportunities to enrich himself a hundredfold, but like Socrates who had refused to beseech his jurors in an effort to save his life, he looked at justice not as a gift to be given and taken by mere humans, but rather as a set of laws that applied equally to all and that upheld the state and therefore civilization itself. We were like that, my family and the people we knew, and the new Mumbai would become increasingly confusing for us to navigate.

Whatever Nilufer Aunty wheedled and coaxed, Kayzad did the opposite. When she and Homi Uncle carefully set the stage for Kayzad to take over the family's thriving law firm, Kayzad casually pronounced one day that he was going to be a doctor. Rashna and I giggled that it was just to spite Nilufer Aunty and that he would go through with it if just for that! Kayzad, Rashna, I, and the assorted servants of the time, ran through the gaping corridors and dusty corners of the flat, stopping only to eat Mamina's fine lunch of *dhan dar,* a turmeric-spiced yellow *dal* with prawn *patio* (prawn-laden tomato and burnt-onion sauce) and delicate side dishes of savory meat pancakes in crisply-tender crusts or *gravy-na-cutlace,* mutton cutlets in divine sweet-spicy tomato gravy. Kayzad chose to eat with us, in another calculated snub at Nilufer Aunty, who pretended not to notice and joined in with her own dishes cooked in her own kitchen by her own trained cook who, it must be admitted, did make the best cheese soufflé in all of India, and with coveted blue-tinned Australian Kraft cheese, not the usual lowly white Amul cheese-cubes, our only indigenous cheese offering of the time. Into Nilufer Aunty and Mamina's on-again, off-again feud, we kids and my mother, who loved the careless and untidy Kayzad as the son she never had and, as we half-heartedly accused her, more than us, resolutely never got drawn. On the day of Kayzad's sober announcement about his future, Nilufer Aunty shrilled louder than usual, perhaps sensing that this was not a joke. "Such a shameless boy! Says he's going to do medicine when his father is waiting for him with a full practice all ready for him!" And, perhaps not too far from the truth: "He just dreams up these things to upset me! What have I done to have such a pig-headed son?" But soon, the prestige of having a doctor (specialist! surgeon!) in the family danced tantalizingly in front of her, took precedence over visions of the lost law pedigree, and salved any hurt.

Years later, after Kayzad became a surgeon and settled in England, he dropped just such a quiet bombshell on his mum and dad. "There's this girl I'm going to marry. Her name is Helen, and she's English." It took months for Nilufer Aunty to recover from the shattered remains of her dreams of the finest Parsi wedding in all of Bombay with the suitable, high-society, full-Parsi daughter-in-law whose family had been carefully vetted and approved by her, for most Parsis were obsessed with only marrying other Parsis in order to prevent the community dying out. But she quickly bounced back, for in socialist India, anything *phoren*, even a bride, was worth its weight in status and prestige.

In the evening, we had tea and biscuits and if we were lucky, fragrant, hot, sweet, puffy *bhakras* of the kind now only sold at one of the last remaining Parsi bakeries, Sir Ratan Tata Institute (RTI), by a version of the impoverished gentlewomen whom the Institute was originally set up to assist. Later, we boarded the old baby-blue Morris Minor and went to Marine Drive for a walk on the promenade. Paps and Mummy being our only drivers in Santacruz, Mamina's uniformed driver made us feel grand. "Take that, you suburbanites with your nouveau-riches," I thought with satisfaction, "this is the real thing—old, tried and true, first class." The old car with its silver trim shone to perfection and certainly beat our boxy, second- or third-hand Fiat into the dust. "Come along, come along," Mamina urged, and we hopped into the car. Kayzad rarely joined us on our evening "outings," having, as he would rudely claim, better things to do. We had come to accept that Kayzad had a heart of gold, but no one could deny that he was and remains utterly without tact or guile.

On Marine Drive, Firi and I tired of walking as the promenade itself was unenlivened by vendors or stalls, a blessed rarity in Bombay, which we of course were too young to appreciate. And the magnificent facades of the art-deco and colonial two-, three-, and (maximum) four-story buildings that lined the sea face we quickly grew bored of, although Marine Drive with its tall lamps creating the Queen's Necklace that brilliantly sparkles to life at night is still one of the finest stretches of road, possibly the finest, we have in Bombay. After an hour of shamelessly peering into the chandeliered flats of the buildings overlooking Marine Drive with singular names like Firdaus, Samudra, Mahal, or Ocean Queen, and drinking *nariel pani* out of coconut shells, and sucking up the soft, slithering scoops of tender coconut, and idly fantasizing about how I was actually walking alongside the Nile in Cairo or the Bosphorus in Istanbul, I pestered Mum and Mamina to go for a horse-ride at the Oval Maidan near Churchgate instead.

In one of the gardens off the Oval Maidan, in a weedy track around a large gazebo that is now long vanished like a Bombay chimera that may or may not have ever been, and hidden under long fronds of greenery, horses were given out for staid rides to kids like us. Vendors of *channa*, peanuts, and *bhel*, stood around as evening goers casually went over for the snacks in paper cones, asking for extra twists of lime, dashes of chili powder, or handfuls of fresh green chilies and coriander to be thrown in. As we approached, thin, undernourished horse-minders in tattered clothes called out loudly the virtues of their animals. "Come, baby, see Raja is best horse. So gentle-gentle!" and, "Giving guarantee, no fall-down with Heera—*arre* double guarantee!" Round and round the gazebo we bounced on an emaciated old nag that was brought out with the promise of an *ekdam*-fine ride, and gleefully shouted out insults to other kid-riders as we passed them by.

Later, we fed the poor old horse with grave solicitude, not seeing the irony of our generosity and concern for this beast even as his hungry and pitiful minder looked on. Mummy and Mamina gazed up at the twinkling lights switching on in the handsome flats flanking the Oval on one side with Bombay University on the other and softly discussed a distant cousin who lived in one of the beautiful flats overlooking the Oval that had belonged to his parents. "Wonder how Medeomah is getting on with that Parveen," Mum mused. "Married the poor fool for his money only." And Mamina, more circumspect, would only allow that she hoped she was taking good care of him.

I knew the flat where we had once paid a duty-visit: old, beautifully appointed with old-world European furniture and the standard heavy, ebonized, and carved Parsi pieces, and dressers full of hand-painted Japanese tea-sets and silver salvers. Its large French doors looked out at the open green-brown expanse of the Oval Maidan where kids played and dog-walkers led their pets. A streaming office crowd purposefully crossed the *maidan* as a shortcut to or from the cacophonous Churchgate station at the end of the western railway line, which transported millions of Bombayites daily from distant suburbs to town and back. Through the windows we could hear the steady, muffled cracks of cricket bats on leather balls and the random shouts of boys putting together an impromptu game, but even these were subdued as if in reverence of the magnificent flats around them. Beyond the Oval, we could see the dark stone buildings of Bombay University looming. We sat around while Parveen dutifully served tea in a delicate Japanware tea-set that Mum would certainly have left in the show-case rather than risk its inevitable breaking, and quite deftly avoided Mum's nosy questions about their affairs, "Parveen, tell me, does Medeomah go to office these days?" or, "What do you do with your whole day?" As Parveen responded evasively, poor Medeomah smiled faintly and nodded agreement with the new wife. "What a *doodh-pao*," Mum sniffed disdainfully later, using the term for someone soft and malleable and of questionable mettle, literally a sopping mess of milk-soaked bread. And with a sigh, "That woman will definitely make short work of all Sorab Uncle's hard earned money."

That flat stood like a jewel in my memory. Indeed, the immaculate old flats of such beautiful visages and exquisite furnishings that had been so well-maintained existing in Bombay, was a revelation even then, when there were surely more of them than what remain today. It was like an airy Parisian apartment, where the air itself rose and floated above the perspiring and sticky existences of the rest of us Bombayites. I asked Mum recently about the flat and Medeomah, and she replied that she had lost touch with them over the years, but that Medeomah had died and God knew what the woman had done with everything.

Back at Khalakdina Terrace, Paps would wait patiently for our return, drinking Scotch with Homi Uncle while Nilufer Aunty, of whose my father was rather a favorite, perhaps because she felt the kinship of long-suffering in-law-dom, plied him with *chavena*, the small plates of nuts and spicy fried bits of puffed rice and dough that accompanied evening drinks. "When will you put some *gos* on your bones, Bomi? You're so thin like a stick, my God!" And she looked smugly down at her own pleasantly round figure, encased in a form-fitting polyester dress ("Marks & Spencer, *dikra* bought this on the last England trip"), the better to show it off by. Once she had proudly pointed out that her ample bosom had not allowed her to see the tips of her toes ever since she had turned sixteen, and poor Gool's thin chest, *bechari* no comparison! As always, Mum had dismissed any such talk coming from any quarter with her usual toss of head and change of subject. It must be remembered that Mummy had a master's in Geography, "M.A, M.Ed," as she would state with finality whenever challenged on any subject—checkmate.

An evening drink—or two—before a drive home was normal and expected and no one would think twice before taking the wheel to start their journey, as long as they felt no effects of the liquor (and often, I am sure, when they might have). Decades later, in the new Mumbai, drunk-driving laws have finally been passed. Of course by now, corruption is so endemic that one may pay one's way through anything, even being caught driving alarmingly drunk, or sometimes even vehicular homicide. Hundred and thousand rupee notes (and there are now so many of these that they are proffered like *paise*—loose change) slyly or openly given and taken allow the offender to proceed unfettered. Only recently have those with money—celebrities, worshiped millionaire and billionaire politicians, Bollywood stars, and cricketers—been apprehended and prosecuted for their actions behind the wheel, including mowing down, like a rogue army Humvee, pavement dwellers as they slept. This augurs well for the new Mumbai but we have, as Nehru was fond of quoting, "miles to go" before order and civility emerge from the current chaos. In any case, my Paps rarely drank more than one whisky.

Returning from our drive, we would burst into the drawing room fresh from our evening out and, seeing the gently smiling Paps waiting patiently, suddenly want to get home while still battling the wrench of leaving Mamina behind. Reality, unheralded—our Santacruz life—had intruded on our day, and we were left to gather our shopping bags, books, and anything else plied onto us by Mamina and make our way to the car for the late evening ride home where, amid other worries of school and home and neighborhood, Mary Lunjen would be waiting with dinner.

If Mamina dreaded our going home, if she lamented her long widowhood in a country that was singularly unkind to widows, she never displayed it, gathering our things and helping move us briskly along into the car to go home as the fluorescent tube lights favored by the Rustoms (Paps would again shake his head in sorrow at the gauche choice made strictly for functionality and not for design in the prosaic Rustom way) harshly flooded the flat and etched my grandmother's face in wrinkles and tiredness that I quickly turned away from.

Chapter 4

WE WERE PARSIS

Fleeing Arab persecution in Persia in small rickety boats, Parsis had, for about a thousand years, lived in cities in Gujrat—Surat, Valsad, Golvad, Navsari, Daman, Diu, and later in Bombay—enriching and being enriched by their new homeland, entwining their ancient Zoroastrian traditions into the framework of Indian life. Parsis loved Bombay, their first and finest home in the world. You see, in India they were not Persians any longer, and later they were not even Iranis, as more recent Zoroastrian refugees to Bombay were termed, having been branded by their place of origin; they had been reborn in India as Parsis (from Pars, Persian, but of India), and so Bombay was indeed their first home, their motherland. Everywhere else they settled after Persia, they had failed to etch their mark into the bones and skin of their new cities. In Europe, they melted into the population and disappeared almost without trace—no monuments, no buildings, no fire-temples, and ultimately no *bawas* or *bawis* (mildly eccentric Parsi misters and misses as Bombayites playfully called them). In Iran, seen as second-class citizens who drew inwards for protection and survival, they had to submit to the will of their new Islamic masters and preferred (and still prefer today) to remain faceless and unseen to avoid persecution.

But in India, they flowered and flourished and sprinkled with gratitude the seeds of their prosperity over their new home. Every Parsi child had heard the story of our arrival on India's western coast in leaky boats, in an arc stretching from Sanjan to Udvada, Navsari, Surat, and Daman and then to Bombay, with many not making the journey from Persia alive. Every child had been told of the generous welcome afforded them by the Hindu king Jadi Rana in Sanjan, Gujrat, allowing refugees freedom and opportunity. The Parsis in turn had made a promise to the king that they would not cause any upheaval in existing life and custom, nor would they try to proselytize: they would be like sugar dissolving in milk, making it sweeter but not causing it to spill over, ever. Indeed, even Parsi names morphed into this cautious Indian-Persian synthesis: while the community kept Persian first names over the centuries, many adopted last names like Patel or Gandhi from Gujrat. Others simply took on last names that echoed their place of birth, like Billimoria; or their trade, like Engineer or Doctor or *Bottlewalla*, the ubiquitous *walla* denoting seller of (in this case) bottles. Many a time my mother expressed open and fulsome gratitude to India for having taken us in. "My girls, here we are blessed to live in freedom rather than in oppression in Iran. Here, we are allowed to do anything." This repeated thankfulness for India's democracy and embrace echoed my uncle Nader's predictable and constant "India is best" refrain as he swore that he had no use for ever stepping foot outside its borders, and never did.

So in Bombay, Parsis built companies that grew into household names and became famous not just for the business that they did in hospitality, ship-building, textiles, and iron and steel, but also for the humane and ethical way in which they conducted it, as they conducted other aspects of life (for instance, a Parsi-owned used car was widely sought after, buyers willing to pay a sort of "Parsi premium" for an assuredly reliable sale). The venerable Tata Company headquartered in Bombay House; Parsi General, Masina, and so many other hospitals all over the city; the Taj Hotel, Grant Medical College, J.B. Vatcha, Petit, Maneckjee Cooper, and innumerable schools that educated generations of children—Bombay was littered with the buildings and monuments that Parsis built for business and philanthropy for the city that took them in. These monuments had something about them that was indescribably Parsi—a timeless air, neoclassical architecture subtly mixed with a Persian aesthetic of wide and curving balconies and imposing columns that together seemed steeped in a symmetrical and orderly past, blending London and Bombay and Persepolis effortlessly and without distraction. A *farohar*, the winged half-human creature in Zoroastrian mythology that Parsis believe to be a *fravashi*, a protective angel of sorts, might grace an entrance or top a building, lending a cosmopolitan elegance that borrowed the best from east and west and made it its own. But by the seventies and eighties, the Bombay of my growing up, our minuscule community was getting much smaller, standing on the cusp of probable extinction in the next century.

In the drawing rooms of my relatives, amid the heavy black lacquered "Parsi" furniture—lavishly carved dressers, *chaise longues,* the inevitable Chinese and Japanese porcelain, tarnished silver, *chinoiserie* (Parsis had traded in China too, primarily Shanghai and Hong Kong, for a thousand years), and, on flaring legs, glass-fronted wooden show-cases filled with ruby red and deep blue Bohemian cut-glass and dusty Staffordshire figurines—Parsis talked with soft regret, tinged with disbelief, about how we were dying out, how the younger generation didn't value the history and traditions that had kept us strong for so many centuries. "They don't wear their *sudras* and *kustis*," they lamented. "*Arre, baba*, who will keep them safe?" Emboldened by my relentless reading I launched into a smug pre-Socratic argument about how *sudras* and *kustis*, linen undershirts and sacred threads and other talismans, could not possibly have anything to do with being safe. I scoffed, "Do you really think that this cloth is what makes the difference between a good Parsi and a bad Parsi? But why, it's just a cloth! If I am a good person, who are you or any *dasturji* or priest to tell me otherwise, just because I don't wear *sudra-kusti*? Only God can tell, *bus*. That's it." And slyly, because I couldn't resist, "if there is a God."

"*Arre, arre, arre, tut tut*," Silloo Aunty would cluck with anxiety at my foolish baiting of the gods. Paps's sister was quite tradition-bound and every evening would light a small *afargan*, a silver miniature of the huge urns that held the sacred fire in our Fire Temples. The most important Fire Temple was in Udwada and held a never-extinguished flame from a Fire Temple in Persia, which had been brought carefully over the oceans by the desperate fleeing Zoroastrians or Zarathushtis. Silloo Aunty, speeding through the rooms of her house with the gently-billowing sandalwood wafting behind her, muttering the *Avesta* prayers under her breath and completing all the rooms at record speed, could not bear to hear any doubts expressed about our religious traditions. Mum would present a sphinx-like façade, because her daughter was really saying what she might have said, but as an adult setting example for children, daren't. Although she (and Paps) believed in a benevolent God (preferably Zoroastrian, Zarathushti, of course, Ahura Mazda himself) who looked over all humanity, above all else she admired outspokenness, rationalism, and a poke in the eye of tradition, even religious tradition. Strangely enough, even Paps from the more traditional Pavri *khandaan*, was distrustful of lavish displays of open religiosity; consequently, our household, though infused with Parsi culture, was never suffused with the intolerant and sexist dictates of dogma and ritual, whether from Zoroastrianism or any other religion, and Rashna and I grew up knowing there were no limits on the questions we could pose.

Other, more absurd conversations, revolved ad nauseam around the wonders we Parsis had wrought despite our small numbers—by the time I left Bombay, we were about 75,000; at our height in India in the 1940s, we had been about 120,000. By 2050, we are projected to be around 35,000, at which point it may not be an exaggeration to say that the flats, monuments, buildings, and charitable trusts of Bombay Parsis will surely outnumber the actual people many times over.

We kids rolled our eyes and mocked, "Of course, we know!" "We built Bombay! *Arre* we were the first doctors and lawyers, and the Tatas are the finest company in the world! Best! Most ethical business model, yes, yes!" "Correct, correct; how did such a small community achieve such greatness!"

But amidst the comedy was a hint of melancholia, a pale grey sheet of the thinnest chiffon like the weightless silver bordered saris my aunties wore to Agiary, which suddenly obscured one's view; a chimera that I couldn't shake. While Parsis were best known for their general jollity and their love of the good life (not necessarily the contemplative, virtuous, classical version, although we did have our fair share of armchair philosophers and many—too many—Shakespeare quoters), and while the clinking of Chivas-filled glasses and loud bombast were as ubiquitous at any gathering as food and laughter, I fought my sense of disconnection and isolation. Who were we, really? Why were we so different, with our olive skins and prominent noses? If we hadn't come to India, where would we now be? More importantly, *who* would we now be? And sometimes: Why couldn't I just have been born a "regular" Indian—an Indian who spoke Hindi fluently, performed *puja* to various deities, who virtuously eschewed beef or pork, didn't have a strange Persian name, and had a "motherplace" somewhere in the bowels or far reaches of India, while we had only Bombay, and whose bona fides were therefore unquestioned, steady and sure, whereas ours were so complicated!

But I also had great admiration and gratitude for my people—so brave to have come so far from the home of their ancestors, to have started again without looking back, and to have left such an outsized footprint on the streets, lanes, and gullies of Bombay. There was a bond between us that allowed me to accept and keep them unquestioningly as mine. In a bus, a restaurant, a park, or at school, I recognized a Parsi in a flash, and as our eyes locked momentarily, we both registered that unspoken tie: We are the same. We have traveled so far, you and I. I know how you feel and how you navigate your life in this city that you also love. The way you know this city, I know this city—we travel together. I know how you look and I am drawn to you because you look like this, like my grandmother and my mother and my aunty and my cousins. We are together in this, you don't know how this long, long journey is going to end, and I feel your anxiety and helplessness, because it is mine too.

Of course, we would then proceed to ignore each other.

Sometimes I pretended to fast or shun meat with my Muslim or Hindu friends. It was so much easier than explaining why my mother might proclaim with relish, "Today we have *bheja* for dinner! So much trouble I had finding fresh-fresh pieces in the market, but my regular *butcherwalla* was saving these *taza-taza* ones for me!" And, with supreme triumph, "We shall have lovely *bheja cutlace* today!" Impossible to explain to fastidious Indian vegetarians that we actually made cutlets and patties (cutlace-pattice!) of soft goat brains mixed with potatoes, spices, and breadcrumbs then fried to a delicate crispy brown, and considered them a great delicacy. More impossible still to describe *gharab*, the fat prosperous sacs of fish roe from the Bhing fish that were seasoned, fried, and then you salted and squirted with lime and ate (how else?) hot-hot.

And I was tired of being judged for the many eccentricities and oddities for which my community was well-known, even if well-loved. For our mothers wearing frocks and skirt-blouses and closed, low-heeled, sensible shoes, and short hair ("Really, your mother has a boy cut?"). For worshiping in quiet, Agiaries, where only Parsis can enter, and plaques declare: Entry Prohibited to Non-Parsis. ("What do you do in there? What is there that we cannot see?"). For my mother relishing cocktails with her friends. (Scandalized: "Your mummy drinks whisky?") For eating offal: kidney, liver, and even, proudly presented, spleen and heart, tossed together with small potatoes in a dish called *aleti-paleti,* whose name itself suggested a certain thrown-togetherness ("*Chee, chee*, you people eat anything!"). For not having a mother-place or father-land or village or starting point within India or even Pakistan. ("But which part of India did your ancestors come from? What's your mother-place?") And always, for our bodies being picked clean by the vultures in the lush tree-laden paradise of Doongerwadi. ("Why, Tinaz, it's so barbaric?!" For this I did not have an adequate response.)

Those vultures are now non-existent in the concrete jungle of Mumbai. The real vultures are the new so-called Parsi leaders who have viciously and deliberately torn apart what remains of our community on new fault lines of who is a real Parsi and whose child can be raised Zoroastrian. In an effort, primarily, to control the considerable funds of a once and still wealthy community, and disguised as attempts to increase and protect our fold and our religion, these charlatans have done more harm to our community than anyone else since the time we arrived in India. Their naked attempts at increasingly stigmatizing those Parsis who, over the years, have mingled with and loved and married other Indians (or simply other human beings anywhere), in the name of our religion, is reprehensible. Ironically, in the new Mumbai, where globalization has inevitably brought so many from different corners of the world into closer contact and is changing what it means to be a Mumbaikar or even an Indian, these Parsi "leaders" have chosen to create new walls around their minds and hearts and to retreat into an imaginary time when we were a "pure" ethno-religious group and community, and therefore presumably able to prosper despite the travails of brutally losing our homeland. They have effectively preyed upon the fears and insecurities of an ever-smaller, ever-older community, some of whose members are heartened by the bluster and ringing denunciations coupled with rosy predictions and palliatives from these leaders.

In my American life, I teach Plato's theory of change in my Political Theory class. We discuss how he examined the questions of reality, existence itself, and acquiring the knowledge of what is real; how he eschewed our lived world, with its impermanence and change, in favor of a constant, unchanging, *real* world. It is a stretch to ask students to disbelieve in what they can see and touch and feel, and to believe in the *idea* of a perfect reality, but we try together to approximate what Plato might have meant in the context of our own rapidly-changing lives.

I think of Bombay, slowly morphing into Mumbai, losing the old anchors of my reality of what it once was: my grandfather's West Breeze-Sea Breeze bungalows within the coconut-tree strewn compound are now six stories taller, the gardens gone, new residents' cars parked over the concrete like ants where once the gardens with flowers and trees and fat caterpillars used to be, and our beloved helpers scattered; Silloo Aunty's ground floor flat, with its wide, curving veranda on the bottom floor of Sea Breeze, where we would sit before the meals were served, with her solidly-proportioned, polished, and surprisingly stylish mid-century modern furniture garnished with the fruits of her crafts everywhere—hand-made Japanese paper lanterns and crocheted doilies—now sold and remodeled beyond recognition (marble/granite/stainless steel); Vera aunty's sprawling, decrepit bungalow next door to West Breeze with its squawking chickens scratching in her back yard now a tall, ugly building filled with strangers; my friends Seema and Priya's top floor abode in Sangeeta Building across from us from which their cries still float downward, hauntingly clear in their sustained pitch and volume that always drove Paps crazy ("*Chee, chee,* how those girls can scream!"), now inhabited by another. If I enter these spaces, will I find the tables and chairs and cupboards and plates, tablecloths and soft, carefully embroidered cushions in intricate patterns that I once touched and admired and held against my face? And if not, can I prove that they once existed? If I cease to remember, will they then never have existed? And if they did exist, do they now matter?

And what about us Parsis? After centuries of building, creating, making, loving, laughing, how will the new Mumbai be without us as this century unfolds? For in less than a hundred years, statisticians calculate that our community will cease to exist. Statistically insignificant, they say, not enough to record. And even though the community rabble-rousers insist that this is a question of faith, and that those who have withstood a thousand years of beating the demographic odds to keep showing up century after century will continue to exist forever, my insistent rationalism, like that of the ancient pre-Socratics who first sought hard evidence as explanation of natural phenomena, is forced in this case to accept the science over simple faith. How then do I live my present life, knowing that the life that made me who I am will be completely non-existent, unidentifiable, a footnote of the past, a mere relic of yore? How do I explain to my children what I have known? Like Diogenes in search of an honest man in ancient Athens, will they later go to Mumbai with a lighted lamp to find evidence of a living Parsi? And not finding it, how will they ever know fully their mother, their Aunty Rashna, the people and places that imprinted us, branded us, made us, and therefore, them?

Chapter 5

WEST BREEZE, SEA BREEZE

Home was the spacious middle flat in West Breeze, one of the two Art Deco buildings my grandfather built in 1930 and into which the family, including my father, the little Bomi, moved from Dina Manzil in the Dadar Parsi Colony. Sea Breeze and West Breeze together comprised a total of five single-floor flats and were surrounded by an enclosed compound that held coconut trees laden with water-bearing fruit (that had to be removed by nimble South-Indian coconut-tree-wallas every three months), scented lemon trees, flowering bougainvillea in fierce reds and purples, and huge white lily bushes on which nested brightly-colored caterpillars. Until the time I was eight, we had flights of dazzling green parrots screech their way of an evening into our gardens and alight on the bougainvillea trees, flashes of pure brilliance—and wonder, because even then they were becoming more and more anomalous in a growing-out-of-control city. All this is now unimaginable, laughable, more evidence of Plato's realm of becoming—everything becoming, surely, something else. The gardens were destroyed when the estate was built up to add more flats and bring income for the sons and daughters of my grandfather, and to expect to see parrots in Mumbai today, except in the still-heavenly Doongerwadi, is an absurdity, so concretized, deflowered, and denuded has the city become.

Above us lived Paps's oldest sister, Amy Aunty, with Nader Uncle and my two cousins, a third having already married and gone to live with her husband. Below our flat was the flat of another of Paps's sisters, Kashmira. She lived abroad with her family and had rented out the flat for a pittance to a Bengali family, whose daughter, Sulaja, became Rashna's fast friend. As part of childhood hierarchy, my friends and I dismissed Sulaja as a younger sister's friend, unworthy of our interest or attention. In the highly class-conscious Bombay society, even a child's pedigree was seemingly determined by an intersection of so many tangibles and intangibles: money was only one factor and did not always triumph as it now often does. Also important, it seemed, were education, family history, the books one read, whether one listened to classical music (Western or Indian were both acceptable), or at least jazz or classic rock or, as a last refuge, pop and disco. Poor Sulaja, a sweet and docile girl who had been adopted by the Bengali couple below, hardly read "our" books which had graduated facilely from Enid Blyton to Man Booker winners and, in what was the final straw, avidly watched Bollywood films, which in those days we dismissively referred to as Hindi movies and never deigned to watch.

Never would I have imagined that in the new India, Bollywood would be elevated to the highest status for so many, or that it would evolve beyond cringe-inducing, over-acted films to a sophisticated machine that now turns out interesting and believable movies that even Gool might watch on extreme rare occasion. Nor that on one recent visit, well-heeled socialites dripping diamonds at Otter's Club's "Eighties Night" would wax nostalgic as they danced enthusiastically to *Baat Ban Jaaye*, which was perhaps the first cross-over Hindi-disco-pop hit that broke as I was leaving India, and helped evolve attitudes of the "smart set" towards Hindi music videos. Nor that Bollywood's stars and celebrities would become Mumbai's greatest obsession (rivaled only by cricketers), and that even Mummy would loudly profess a grand fondness for the madly successful, almost God-like superstars, Sharukh and Amir Khan. Of course, Amir she had taught at Bombay Scottish, and they had sometimes played tennis together at Khar Gymkhana, even after his super-stardom—actor and teacher united over a love of tennis, a school, and a shared past.

Upstairs, my cousins were all more than a decade older, a different generation, less "modern," more old India than even Rashna and I. We eighties children thought ourselves so cool and our friends so hip that cousins invariably receded to the periphery of Pavri potluck lunches and enforced parties that my Aunties unfailingly organized, and that we attended outwardly reluctant but with secret pleasure and anticipation. Of those parties, it must be said that we enjoyed almost as much the ensuant post-party gossip—who made what, how much effort must have been spent on the fish curry ("big-big pieces there were, and the flavor so complex!") or Russian salad ("delicious, but all vegetarian, not a *gos* to be found"—and *gos*, mutton, being indispensable in the gastronomical universe of carnivorous Parsis!) that each family made, whether what was worn was in style or not (none could compare with ours, of course)… shamefully low-minded chitter-chatter like that that Paps never, ever indulged in and actively discouraged. Sometimes, seeing him detached from our party postmortems, Mum would furiously whisper, only half-joking, "See how that man favors them over me," and we would shush her and quickly change the subject, wanting none of the side-choosing that she was forcing. Adults were so tedious when they tried to draw us into their world! Much better that they should stay among themselves and never involve us.

These cousins and relatives were also as obedient and diligent as I was contrary, smart-mouthed, and defiant (but only to Mum and Paps—to the rest of the relatives, as they often remarked, I was such a *gareeb gai*, mild and gentle as a cow). Children in India succumbed to the pressures of society and tradition and had perfected the art of acting the model child in public; in private, it was a different matter, and the decorum could be dropped. In the heavy, languorous afternoons as Mum napped, I would hear my cousin Jasmine, who was an exceptional and assiduous pianist, struggling with her piano practice, stabbing at the keys to coax from them a Brahms waltz, the strains of which wafted briefly and then died until it was retried again and again, the legato abandoned for a rare desperate crashing. We always loved to hear Jasmine through the ceiling, listening to the pieces that we knew later won prizes at competitions. In these uncommonly discordant moments Mum would sigh heavily. "Poor girl is trying," she'd say. "*Bechari* Jasmine!"

Although many of the Pavri women had excelled in music and the sciences, earning Ph.D. and M.B.B.S. degrees, and embarking on lives of research that co-existed easily with the life of the home, their accomplishments were more quietly obtained than those of the Rustoms—rowdy intellectuals, opera buffs, emancipated women, and upper-crust socialites from South Bombay, all excessive and bold; whereas the Pavris were more traditional and deferential. In any case, for Mum to have commented on anyone's piano-playing was astonishing in its boldness, for when she opened the lid of our old ebonized piano to play for the pre-school kids she taught at home after her retirement from high school geography, many started crying and their mothers winced, so out of key was the loudly and robustly-played "Colonel Bogey March," "Roll out the Barrel," and other tone-deaf atrocities from another era. Decades later in my American life, I heard the Brahms No. 15 played again, this time in my eleven-year-old's Suzuki violin group. As the memories of those afternoons in West Breeze rushed to the fore, I turned away from his puzzled scrutiny and forced a smile at his concern. In my American life, Bombay always intruded.

Some of those sultry afternoons where the curtains would be drawn against a punishing sun and the heat hung in a moist and stifling haze, I simply spent doing nothing, walking around the silent flat on bare feet, the old, deep-colored, geometrically-set stone tiles feeling cool and delicious against my hot feet, fans softly whirring in all the rooms in a desperate strategy to create a cross-breeze. I would touch the arm of a chair, tracing a curve down the smooth golden wood of the stylish twin chairs designed by Paps for his own marriage ceremony and on which the bridal couple had sat as the *dastur* chanted prayers, or feel the sharp edges around the deep indigo cut-glass bowl that I remembered from Mamina's showcase at Khalakdina Terrace. Sometimes, as Mum napped, I would sit with my chin on the windowsill and gaze out onto the lane, staring at the listlessly moving branches, looking at Sangeeta Building for signs of life from my friends or at the dozing corner *sabziwala,* who had "closed" his handcart for an impromptu siesta, just idly dreaming away the afternoon. These moments of pure reflection and contentment I have failed to replicate in my American life, where the day never seems to have a rhythm, to slow down and then speed up again, where no siestas are taken, no cues are given to decelerate or start up again, and where doing nothing seems to go against the Puritan strain of industriousness that runs through the day and fuels the guilt of indolence. But when I return, I can recapture these moments with ease, walking like a ghost over the brilliant tiles and noting with rueful satisfaction that not much has changed in any of the rooms of my childhood apartment, even as everything, and everything around it has been transformed.

Next door in Sea Breeze, the ground floor flat belonged to my grandparents (and later Silloo Aunty and Jamshed Uncle) who were taken care of by Paps's brother's family dwelling in the upstairs flat. This large family consisted of Kobad Uncle, Ketty Aunty and five cousins, three brothers, and two sisters, who although a decade older than I, were my greatest cheerleaders. Both flats were connected by a carved wooden staircase, the banisters of which shone from polish and the hurrying hands that had gripped them over the years. When the heavy, exterior side door to the building was locked, the staircase would become an internal one and the two flats would become one big house and their various internal doors could stay wide open. I always thought this great heavy side door an excellent bar in the case of riots or *morchas* or other disturbances (usually over some religious or ethnic slight) that happened with a banal regularity, and made me wonder about the precariousness of our own existence made prominent by our Parsiness. I was glad for the security of a hefty wooden door and the freedom—from societal rage, injury, accident, insult—it afforded within.

Over this staircase my cousins flew up and down to be with Grandpappa and Grandmamma and their old retainers. Grandmamma Sera was paralyzed on one side, but cheerfully and deftly negotiated books, food, and dressing with her good, left side. Her long-time maid, Sita, was devoted to her care and on hot days when the power went out (again!), Sita would dutifully fan my grandma, over her protests, with a large wooden *punkha,* and we sweat-drenched kids would scurry to try to catch the delicious wafts of air being moved about even if momentarily. In the evenings, the many-talented Sita made *rotlis*, thin, piping-hot flatbreads, for the night's dinner. We hovered around the kitchen, trying to steal as many as we could without being noticed. It would invariably be Manek, the youngest of the five, who was caught, sheepishly taking the blame for us all.

Sita and Rama, improbably named after the popular Hindu deity-couple, lived in the two-roomed building in the back of the Sea Breeze and West Breeze compound with their family, which would eventually include children and grandchildren. Rama was a deft carpenter, and was often called upon to undertake projects in all of our homes. When Paps saw the new built-in style furniture taking over in the design world and the flats of his friends, Rama would be summoned. Paps sketched the liquor cabinet he wanted made, complete with mirrored interior, cleverly hinged doors, and shelves for his collection of decanters, bottles, and wine and whisky glasses, and Rama got to work. This new cabinet was then fitted in between our old ebonized piano and carved sofas, creating a strange and eclectic look that Mummy roundly condemned. "Look at what he has done! Cramming that ugly cabinet next to my lovely old piano. How does it look! No sense that man has, really!" Paps would fight back, mildly: "One has to improve the house and do new things! Look at DM-Uschi's flat, how they maintain it! Your mummy can't understand anything about décor, she was used to living in *tabelas*." The horse stable reference, of course, was a barely-veiled insult to the mile-high ceilings of both Khalakdina Terrace and Palamkot Hall. Many a time he had expressed the opinion, to Mum's open derision, that if it had been up to him, he would have installed false ceilings in both flats without delay to banish the barrenness imposed by such tall ceilings and to create a "sleek" (favored word of Bomi at the time when mid-century modern was giving way to a sort of universal eighties cosmopolitan minimalist aesthetic) interior look.

Maintenance of the house was high on Paps' list but featured very low in Mum's universe. The glassware in his new cabinet Paps lovingly washed, dried, and arranged himself because he didn't want Mary, who was invariably clumsy, breaking his collection, and to have expected Mum to have done so would have been unrealistic. As she was fond of saying loudly and repeatedly, a woman's place was not in the kitchen. Eventually, decades later, Paps would give up and the house would fall into a gentle decline, liquor cabinet, piano, dusty cut-glass vases, and oxidizing silver frozen in amiable and dispirited coexistence.

This was one of the many things Mum and Paps disagreed and constantly (sometimes amiably, sometimes sharply) bickered about. A view held by one of them invariably had a very different interpretation by the other. Gool loved her parties, but Bomi held her back. She was devoted to tennis (and still is, regularly feted by the club and getting her picture taken with tennis luminaries, like her favorite Leander Paes, whom she professes to be humble and sweet), but Paps derided the Khar Gymkhana and would barely set foot in it. He longed for her to be more domestic, to make *bhakras*, to cook a special *dal* or *pulao*, and to serve it with care in gleaming dishes instead of throwing it on the table (and secretly, so did I, although I would never admit it), but Gool never stayed still, buzzing in and out of the flat like an intoxicated and exhausting bumblebee.

But in other, important things, Mum and Paps were of the same mind. Both loved classical music with passion, and Mum was greatly proud of Paps's having played violin with the fledgling Bombay Philharmonic Orchestra. After independence, when the British did their vanishing act from India, the orchestra transitioned from primarily English players to Indians, many of them Anglo-Indian, Christian, and Parsi. Going to the Orchestra was the favorite of Parsi dowagers in their pearls and diamonds, and the lack of cultural life in the newly-independent country left impoverished by the British, was routinely lamented within the community. When Paps played in it, the orchestra had Dominic Pereira as first violinist (later, when we girls were taken to concerts, this position would be held by Siloo Panthaki whom we immediately associated with our own Silloo Aunty). The famous cellist, George Lester, incredibly reigned continuously through Bomi's time to the days of our growing up, and we imagined a young and dashing Bomi bowing his heart out on the stage as Lester and the orchestra played. At parties and potlucks, Paps was in demand to bring out the violin and effortlessly play Dvořák's Humoresque or some light Mozart air—because anything more serious would not have been appreciated amid the babble of gathered aunties, uncles, and friends. Then, Mum would close her eyes and smile and be at one with her husband, even if ever so briefly.

Both Mum and Paps were instinctively ethical, without a formal intellectualization of ethical and moral conduct. In a city where even then corruption had seeped into the lives of so many and on so many levels, Paps must have been one of the last Bombay architects who never paid bribes to the Bombay municipality to get his drawings approved, and as a result, never really stood a chance of succeeding wildly. To him, that would have been a trade-off he could not imagine. Mum's views of humanity encompassed all Indians, the poor and recourse-less, Hindus, Muslims, Parsis, everyone. At the height of her pre-school's success, she insisted on throwing its doors open for the education of children in the neighboring slum. I remember the first woman from its huts stepping hesitatingly into our living room with a wide-eyed three-year-old girl wearing an ill-fitting skirt and blouse in tow. My mother urged her to sit like any other parent would, gave her forms to fill and quoted a fee dramatically lower than what was usually charged. Middle-class mothers eventually began to complain about kids from the slums becoming their own children's classmates. "Mrs. Pavri, why are you allowing these children in your school? They are bringing diseases with them and slowing down the whole class!" My mother stood her ground and told them evenly that all children deserved a chance and that without education, India would never progress. Many parents pulled their children out of her pre-school in protest, but Gool kept the school open to everyone to the end even though it meant that enrollment eventually dropped and one day the school had to be closed.

Neither parent ever evoked religious demagoguery in a city, and country, where such name-calling and malicious stereotyping was easy to fall into and where many, both educated and not, across every religious group did. They always underlined a reasoned, inclusive approach to religion which started with the premise that all were equal and that it was much more important to be a *good* person than a religious person. These beliefs did not always find easy echo in a land that was rife with self-styled *sadhus, sanyasins, imams, gurus, dasturs* and other appeasers of the gods, gods that were jealously demarcated as "ours" or "theirs" and that could start riots that resulted in injury and death at the smallest of perceived slights and provocations.

When in childish hubris I mocked the many illiterate masses who believed in spirits and demons and worshiped, what seemed to my mind (filled as it was with the rationalism of voracious reading without the benefit of the wisdom of years), laughable objects, my mother said simply, "Don't make fun of people who believe, Tinaz-*baebee*, because even if they are worshiping a rock, for that moment their mind is on higher things. And it is the higher things that bring out the best in us—how we strive to get to them is not important." I've never found a more convincing explication of the power of faith.

Later, my Aunt Silloo and her husband Jamshed came to live with my aging grandparents on the ground floor of Sea Breeze. Jam Uncle, a dashing "shippee" in his day, a first engineer in the merchant marine, had retired and they had to give up their spacious flat in Mazagon Docks where many a Christmas party, complete with fake Santa (one of the drivers, all dressed up) and bon-bons (which we kids broke open delightedly to find the useless little plastic trinkets within), had been held for all of us nieces and nephews in the vast compound of their multi-building complex. It was thus that *passay* (next-door), either upstairs or downstairs, and *upar* (above) became my refuge. When I was tired of Mum's shrill commands, Paps's censoriousness and general repression, or just needed the constant, unspoken, and waiting warmth of aunties, uncles, and older cousins, I slammed the front door shut and fled, announcing I was going *upar* or *passay*.

Next door, Silloo Aunty would await with a sort of high tea. When Jam returned home in the evening from his land job, they had taken to having a late tea and early dinner all-in-one, a big departure from their stylish ways in Mazagon Docks where lavish dinner parties would never have allowed for such a plebian and functional melding of meals. Now, the table was spread with the meat and vegetables from the dinner as well as the toast, cheese, and cake from the tea. "Ummm Kraft cheese, Silloo Aunty?" I would breathe. "Yes, *dikra*, eat, eat," she would urge. That particular Kraft cheese was not American, but Australian. Purchased in deep-blue tins from the smugglers, because importing most foreign things was prohibited, this was the most coveted cheese in Bombay, never mind Camembert, Stilton, or Roquefort. Mum, who considered herself quite a cheese connoisseur, said she only ate the English cheddar brought by her cousin each winter in large quantities (one whole suitcase always held cheeses, chocolates, hams, and bacons to give away to extended family and friends), but I had seen her cutting hunks of the creamy, yellow Australian Kraft out of its blue tin and popping it into her mouth when she thought she was not being observed.

In households all over Bombay, foreign relatives were repeatedly asked sheepishly or bold-facedly for the two most coveted things from abroad: cheese and chocolate (a strong third was Scotch, but this was strictly limited by the government and one could get in trouble if caught with more than two bottles of alcohol at customs). Our domestic cheese was considered vastly inferior, although over the years I imagine that many, like I, developed a fondness for the bland, slightly salty taste of the unimaginative, white, Amul cheese cubes. These I now buy in the Indian grocery store in my American city, seeking tastes of childhood that bring waves of memories of Paps, the die-hard Indian nationalist, stubbornly proclaiming the superiority of this cheese over all others, and us girls loudly and gleefully shouting him down in our girl-dominated household, as we often did on so many things, "Paps, you're so silly! This cheese is so bad! You don't know anything!"

Sometimes Sorab, Amy Aunty's son, joined us for tea at Silloo-Jam's. Sorab suffered from a deteriorating cerebellar ataxia and could only walk with a swaying gait that became increasingly unsteady in his adulthood. Relatively rare diseases such as these seemed uncommonly frequent in us Parsis, (in fact I knew at least two other more distant relatives with the same affliction), and the word was that our small numbers meant marriage and reproduction in ever smaller circles, thereby raising risks of graver genetic ills for us all. Of the scientific veracity of this I am not certain, but many Parsis seemed to believe and accept it as one more consequence of their uniqueness and rarity and even seemed perversely quite proud of it.

On these occasions at Silloo's, I inwardly, petulantly fretted that I wouldn't have my aunt and uncle (and the goodies from the tea) to myself, especially since I had so efficiently dispatched Rashna when she had enquiringly and hesitantly come over. Later, I came to see Sorab's good-natured ambling through the horrors that life had bestowed upon him as something close to heroic. While he still could, he studied homeopathy, ran a small book shop in Mahim purchased for him by his supportive parents, and tried to live—and for the most part, *did live*—the semblance of a normal life, always without any trace of self-pity. Of course, the unconditional love of his parents and sisters must have made the blow much softer, but could not have erased it. Silloo Aunty constantly asked his advice on a variety of homeopathic alternatives for a cold or a bruise or general forgetfulness and Sorab would confidently prescribe Arnica or Kali Phos, the latter being "best for a sharp brain and preserving your memory, Silloo Aunty." Homeopathic, herbal, and ayurvedic alternatives my mother would loudly pooh-pooh as only allopathic medicine seemed to have been recognized in the Rustom household. "What is homeopathy, just some sugary pills? Don't know why the Pavris believe in these silly things!" But we kids were convinced as to the power of homeopathy, and went running to Silloo for a spoonful of healing Arnica solution when we fell and grazed our elbows or sprained our ankles.

When Paps took us to school in the morning, Sorab sometimes stood at the Linking Road bus stop near our house waiting for the big red BEST buses that would take him to his lonely vigil at his shop (which probably never made much money but at least surrounded him with the warmth of books); it was always a wrench to decide whether to stop, and risk Sorab falling over trying to get to our car through the restless waiting crowds, or to continue onwards, and leave poor Sorab to the travails of the BEST buses, where I imagined he would surely be pushed and shoved and perhaps fall anyway. In reality, Bombay must have taken care of Sorab in the way that it had: of finding compassion amid the grit and hardship, lending a helping hand even amidst the overwhelming needs of its millions.

I never saw Sorab utter a bitter or self-pitying word even as his body failed him more and more and the falls became more regular and sudden, unheralded swoons made his legs buckle and give way. In a country where physical disability was, and is, grossly misunderstood, openly stared at, and often associated with inauspiciousness by the illiterate and superstitious, Sorab had a most visible and unusual impairment, one that was impossible to ignore. But he successfully ignored it, gently poking fun at himself, joining in the good-natured ribbing that came his way from relatives and friends, and always asking others about themselves in an effort to deflect attention away from his situation.

I think he must have been very, very grateful for the solicitous Silloo Aunty (whom we affectionately called whatever we could think of, Silloo, Loo-sil, Silly Sil), who reserved a time for him during each week and made him a lovely tea. It was "Sorab's day," Silloo would cluck anxiously, her salt and pepper curls always gleaming from the Wella silvering hair treatment that sister Kashmira regularly brought from abroad, and thinning eyebrows arched and penciled to perfection, and he would "be here any minute." Then, we could start tea, but never before. Silloo, who did not have children of her own, was kind and generous like that, embracing us nieces and nephews in her soft, comforting arms which had never held biological children but had given so much warmth and love. Most of all, she claimed Jamshed's brother's children as her own, and brought them faithfully from Colaba to Santacruz to spend most weekends. And of these three she loved Firdaus best, whose brittle bones cracked like twigs and whose little legs never grew properly, and who later became my confidante, "friend, philosopher and guide," as my boyfriend, the Engineer, had once said with amusement and scorn and perhaps a little jealousy.

Passay upstairs, my five cousins lived in the kind of acrimonious harmony that five siblings will necessarily create. Kobad Uncle, my expansive, jolly, larger than life, hardy-esque uncle beamed with pleasure when I climbed up that flight of wooden stairs to the first floor, and rang the doorbell. "Come, *dikra*, come," he gestured. "My Tinaz has come," he would bellow while I shyly slipped in and looked around for the cousins. Anahita and Arnavaz already worked in offices in town, and their purses, shoes, and office clothes were so elegant to my young eyes. Often, Arnavaz would open her Godrej cupboard and picking up a small bottle of perfume or nail-polish out of the inner compartment, would press it into my hand saying, "Take, take, I have so many!" And I would sniff at the bottle in delight, not knowing that in fact she didn't have so many, that everything she and they had was hard-earned, unlike in our household where Rashna and I seemed to get everything we wanted, and because of that were always very careful to ask for very little.

Often, I would spend the night in the warmth of my cousins' large nest, much to the puzzlement of Mum. "Why do you want to go there, darling?" "What is there?" "What do you all talk about there, what do you do with them?" Mum's possessiveness showed up in ways, both expected and unexpected, perhaps a result of her having to be separated from Mamina at such a young age to go live with Roda Aunty while poor Mina with all her challenges became the increasing focus of her mother's attention.

I never explained that *passay* upstairs, I felt safe, welcomed and cherished as if I were the star, my accomplishments at school inquired after and celebrated by my uncle and aunty. "*Wah, wah,*" they would exclaim in delight, "see Tinaz is getting all first class marks and came fourth in her whole class again! Such a clever girl she is!" When I spent the night, we sat up and listened to *Top of the Pops* on the radio until midnight and Arnavaz sang along to the tunes in her high, mellifluous voice that, bird-like, never hit a wrong note and would surely have made it big as one of the ubiquitous thin voiced back-up singers of plaintive Hindi film songs if Parsis had just known about such things back then. Decades later, Parsis would beam with pride at Penaz Masani who had made it big in the Indian classical world, playback singing in numerous Bollywood films, her achievement quite unusual and exciting in a community dominated by pianists and violinists.

The songs we listened to on *Top of the Pops* were already one or two years old in the West but were most exciting for us in India, having just arrived. This was the only radio program on the only existing, (and that too government-owned) radio channel, All India Radio, that played English songs, and we all waited week after week to hear them. Arnavaz was also known to take up the mike without self-consciousness at countless *navjotes*—coming of age Zoroastrian ceremonies—and Parsi weddings, and unerringly belt out "Somewhere My Love," "Autumn Leaves," "Killing Me Softly" or later, at our insistence because those other songs were so old, "*Hasta Manana*" from Abba. Indeed, so well-known was Arnavaz's singing that she was invariably demanded as soloist by relatives and guests, and Nellie of Nellie and the Band, the most famous of *navjote* bands, woman powered with mother and daughter at the helm, would graciously acquiesce and the crowd would roar its approval.

So Arnavaz took the lead during our Saturday night shindigs at Sea Breeze upstairs. Manek, the youngest, who was short and rotund, would shake his round bottom and try to drown out the song session in wild mimicry. Then his siblings would all descend on him with the nonsense verse,

> Manek makori,
> ghadial ni takori,
> ghadial vaje ding, ding,
> Manek nache ting, ting.

> Absurdly:
> Manek is an ant
> on the hands of a clock;
> the clock goes ding, ding
> while Manek dances ting, ting.

I would feel my heart softening for poor Manek, who at that moment seemed to have no friends among his siblings, and who I knew was not always very focused on his studies because he had secretly shown me his report card of which it could only be said that much work needed to be done that year. This would prompt one of my many conversations and bargains with God, offering that I would gladly lose a place even in the top ten in my class, let alone top three, if only, only, Manek could pass that year with flying colors. Somewhere God must have heard my pleas, because Manek is a successful, driven entrepreneur in the new India, becoming a sought-after chef and restaurateur and in the bargain, making Ketty Aunty's fabulous recipes for prawn curry and *dhansak*, the single-most famous Parsi dish in India, a rich dark sweet-spicy lentil curry crammed with tender pieces of mutton served over rice browned with caramelized sugar, legendary all over Bandra.

In the morning after a sleep-over, Ketty Aunty would be busy in their large, un-remodeled, old-fashioned stone kitchen with a walk-in *mori* within to facilitate a large-scale washing-up of various-sized copper-bottomed *tapelas* and dishes, whipping up scrambled eggs. The irresistible smell of the strong chicory coffee wafted to the mattresses in the living room where we cousins slept all in a row. When we ran out of eggs, the cousins would go without seconds, but I would be urged to eat more. "Come on, eat, otherwise you won't grow bigger. So thin you are!" I would see Manek eying the eggs hungrily but under Ketty Aunty's watchful eye, he would slide the plate to me over my protests.

I would give anything to return to that flower and tree-filled compound of warmth and happiness, to go to another potluck and discover what my aunties had cooked, to savor Ketty Aunty's gently-scrambled eggs made creamy with milk, to listen with anticipation to *Top of the Pops*, to careen up and down flights of wooden stairs to see my cousins in West Breeze and Sea Breeze, to exist contentedly at the edges of an adult world that offered complete safety, acceptance, and love as a banality of daily existence. In my American life, I lament that my boys will never know what this kind of living was like, how strengthening and nurturing it was to be tightly encircled by so many people you knew loved you unquestioningly. How magical was our bougainvillea-bedecked haven in West Breeze, Sea Breeze! So I tell my boys the stories and hope that they will be enriched anyway, through the weight of ancestral ties and the osmosis of unstated familial love that will reach out and touch them through the decades and continents.

Chapter 6

SANGEETA BUILDING

Across the lane from our home in West Breeze stood a boxy Art Deco building with three stories. Each held three capacious flats with a boldly-designed column on the right, within which ran up the broad flight of stone-and-tile stairs to each flat. Over these stairs I ran, two at a time, over a period of more than a decade, to my friends' flat on the top floor. Our area of Khar-Santacruz held an unusually high number of such buildings, built, as was ours, in the 1920s, 30s and 40s, some with more pronounced Art Deco features than others. Some were single homes, bungalows; others, like ours and Sangeeta building's, were one big flat to a floor, almost unheard of now, rare even then. Lining Linking Road, for instance, is now a main north-south artery of the city, beginning in Bandra and extending to Juhu and beyond, were bungalows, and square, round, and angular buildings with the familiar hallmarks of the period: geometric symbols embossed into the facades, curving balconies, linear stairways, and pastel washes of faded paint. They also abounded in our own Banyan- and Gulmohor-tree-lined residential area in the lanes and gullies off the main Linking Road. Many were enclosed in walled compounds and held gardens lesser or more within the thick rounded whitewashed plaster walls. Others fronted Linking Road, which was not a problem decades ago, but certainly unfortunate now with the relentless crush of non-stop traffic, dirt of non-stop construction, the tread of non-stop footsteps, and the twenty-four-seven nature of city life.

On the top floor of Sangeeta Building with its enormous balcony (later enclosed in glass to form a third, much needed bedroom that exuded shine and glamour in the tired building frame) and open terrace attached to the flat, lived my friends, Seema and Priya, along with their older sister Vibha. Inevitably brought together in an impromptu neighborhood game of hide and seek when we were barely five, they became my earliest and fastest friends. With Seema and Priya, I trolled our neighborhood lanes and gullies, whiling away time, gathering new friends and acquaintances later to be discarded like the stones we collected and threw away for our desultory hop-scotch games on the lane between our homes as new buildings began to spring up around us. I always jealously guarded my relationship with these two, afraid that new upstarts would disturb our perfect friendship which had been cemented over neighborhood familiarity, gossip, dolls, boys, endless trips to the corner *bania* shop to buy sweeties and candies and sugar cigarettes with flame-red ends that we stuck insouciantly in our lips, complaints about parents (more mine than theirs) who just didn't understand dreams, desires, and hopes. I needn't have worried, however, because in the fifteen years that we spent together before I left, through our respective schools and colleges, and while Priya picked a neighborhood boy for marriage, and their sister Vibha became an Air India stewardess (so glamorous, back then in socialist India, enough to make even me forget about America for a while!), our friendship always stood the test of newcomers, outsiders, and gate-crashers, picking up seamlessly where we left off each day, week, month, or year.

These were my neighborhood friends. So important, so comforting to come home to from the rigors of Bombay Scottish, where I worked furiously and hard in all my subjects but was always nipped for first, second, and third place in the class by kids who were driven more, studied more, and perhaps had parents who pushed harder while mine hardly seemed to mind. My strivings were ever propelled by the one goal that became my fixed nirvana: to get a scholarship so that I could go to the America of my imagining. I imagined a life in America free of the confines and dictates of family, tradition, and the tight bonds of a city I'd known since birth. I longed for America's independence, individualism, and even its willingness to leave one alone. So much did I study compared to my neighborhood friends and, more sacrilegiously still, so much did I care about my studies that I was unceremoniously nicknamed "mugpot" by the neighborhood gang, a moniker I hated and tried to shrug off by exuding greater nonchalance and an air of studied unscholarliness, fibbing about not studying at all, and wailing at every available opportunity like countless other Indian kids (even the brainiest), "I'm going to fail Math/Geography/Physics/Biology tomorrow!" In India, kids never claimed to have "aced" a test, or to have done "amazingly," or admit to even being remotely prepared for any exam. These confident assertions I only encountered in America later, with some surprise. In India, we were always "going to fail," even when we fully expected to score very, very well. And mugging, cramming an ocean of facts and data into every crevice of your brain, was the name of the game.

In the evenings after school, on weekends, on bank holidays, which included a vast number of religious observances for Jains, Buddhists, Hindus in all their regional variations, Muslims, Christians, and Parsis (before they made Navroz an optional holiday, perhaps in late recognition of our dwindling numbers—it was kind of silly to give hundreds of millions an off day because some seventy thousand Parsis were celebrating an ancient start of spring) and in the short holidays—Diwali, Christmas, and Michaelmas—my friends and I were inseparable.

From their terrace on the second floor of Sangeeta, Seema and Priya's voices would ring out shrilly and ear-splittingly, "Teeeeeeenaz!" Paps would wince and cover his ears exaggeratedly. "Arre, again those girls are screaming! Are you really going to go over there again? Why every day, what do you do there?" Because for Paps, having his daughters home where he could watch over them was a daily goal (though rarely achieved). Mum would whisper with glee, "Go, go, *dikra*, have fun. Go with Seema-Peema." Because in her slightly mad way, Mum never could or would remember any of our friends' names and usually created a crazy rhyme or alliteration that approximated what they might be. This new Mum-given nomenclature all my friends gladly and proudly accepted, wearing it like a badge of honor, but I roundly condemned and accused her of forgetting on purpose for attention's sake.

For the Rustoms, getting dressed in the evenings and "going out to have fun" was most important. Sometimes, it could be an oppressive dictate for us. Come evening my mother would begin to fidget and get restless if she couldn't go to the Khar Gymkhana where she was a regular at tennis, and where she still plays after fifty years and is recognized and feted as a "tennis elder." Even the visiting Roda Aunty, if she saw me lingering at home on an evening when the friends were not around, would ask as if shocked, "Not going outside? No friends today? Why are you staying home in the evening, slinking around, *chee chee baba*, go out and play in the fresh air!" (Because of course she couldn't be expected to say go out and play in the fetid, humid, oppressive air, even though this is what Bombay air was, nothing fresh about it at all, ever).

While Rashna grinned and became invisible in the way she had perfected, I would mumble something about going later and fade away until Mum and Roda had safely left for their obsessive, evening's "going out." This could be to the Gymkhana, some cursory shopping in Khar where they would pick up some mutton patties or small cakes to bring home for evening coffee, or to actually go have coffee in one of the small Bandra cafés or modest Juhu beach-front hotels, the few five-stars in Bombay being much more of a splurge than they would ever consider for a casual evening, not that there were any five-stars in our suburbs at that time anyway. If it were a weekend, Paps would join them, an improbable but perfectly amiable threesome, Mum, Paps, and Roda Aunty, united through marriage, routine, and the perfect coinciding of social norms, expectations, and experiences.

Now, Mum and Paps rarely eat out, so expensive has the new Mumbai become and so principally against spending that kind of money are they. Glitzy new restaurants adorn the pot-hole-filled roads and alleys, but their prohibitive prices and exotic globalized fare ("Thai fusion, *baebee*? What rubbish is that—whatever happened to proper good food? No-no we are staying at home only, eating the lovely food cooked by Prerna") only underline for my parents that the Bombay they (and I) knew is transformed in new and different ways each day.

In the evenings, we friends would gather another friend, Ganesh, from the first floor of Sangeeta building and then proceed to make good-natured fun of him until he would be rescued, or further tormented, by other boys from close-by buildings from down the lane: Dilip, Akash, and Akhil. Sometimes we would be joined by Raja and Rani, an absurdly-named king and queen brother-sister duo who had just moved into a newly-built bungalow, impressive for its elegant fittings, expansive lawns, and gardens where the parents sat regally for tea or drinks. It was also impressive because by then no one built new bungalows anymore, and the first of the existing bungalows, like Vera Aunty's next door, had already started to make way for new high-rise buildings all along our narrow lanes. These two siblings each had well-designed rooms with en suite bathrooms and phones in each room, coveted luxuries for me, for I had to share my room with Rashna while Mum ran her nursery, a pre-school converted out of our large would-be third bedroom, and I certainly didn't have a phone in my room; for over a decade of my life we hadn't even had a phone in our home as the waiting list for new lines seemed interminable. I always feared that Seema and Priya would gravitate away from me towards such open displays of wealth and unmistakable whiffs of *phoren* money, but these other neighborhood friends came and went, while our friendship endured.

By six in the evening we would all be gathered around the curved corner compound wall of Sangeeta, watching the *tamasha* that the crossroads in front of us brought to our view each day, a spectacular montage of traffic, hangers-on, walkers, dogs, familiar regulars, and unfamiliar passers-by. From that perch, I would see my *passay* cousins coming home to Sea Breeze or leaving to go out again. Beyond a quick wave, I would never venture towards them; my friends and I were a separate world, one that in my teen-aged angst and eternal state of embarrassment I feared could not easily mix with the robust Parsiness of my relatives. As dusk settled and lights went on in flats around us, we saw Sorab lumbering back from work or Paps pulling into West Breeze's gravel driveway in his old Fiat—old, familiar, close-by things that somewhere within me I registered with deep and unspoken satisfaction and gratitude. Paps I always studiously ignored just as I did Mum, who returning from tennis at Khar Gymkhana in an inappropriately short-short skirt and waved gaily in a way that made my humiliation complete. Boys and girls from next-door lanes would join us at the wall, and we would be as inviting or rejecting as their place in our social hierarchy warranted.

Across from the wall, the busy Ramakrishna Mission Road that crossed over the much busier Linking Road led further down to the Ramkrishna Temple, which sat serenely in front of a pond in which goldfish swam and lotuses floated. Here we would spend an evening, sitting for the end of the *bhajans* led by orange-clad monks for a few minutes, and then get in line for the *prasad*, sweet offerings at the end of the service that we crammed in our mouths and went back for shamelessly. Leaving the temple, we would pool together our coins, and from the *golawalla* outside buy *golas*, dipping the crushed-ice balls in their exotic syrups of watermelon, *kalakhatta* (sweet-sour grape?), lemon-lime, intensified with a special salty masala sprinkled on them. Then we would stagger back home, another evening's trolling complete.

The *bhel-puriwalla* set up his cart across the wall at seven exactly. *Bhel-puri* carts were and are ubiquitous around the city. The street food that Bombay cannot do without, *Bhel-puri* is made up of different variations of puffed rice, thin, fried straws of *sev*, and disks of crisp, deep-fried flour that constitute the crunchy *puri*, paired with chopped onion, cilantro, potatoes, and a mélange of sweet and hot chutneys as toppings. It is craved by all Bombayites and indeed available to all prosperous businessmen rubbing shoulders with domestic servants at the *bhel-puri* carts. This particular *bhel-walla's* fame had spread in our area so that hungry locals lined up at the spot quickly, and we raked the crowd over with a critical eye, deciding who should be dismissed (most of them) and who were worthy of further conversation (neighborhood peers whose clothes or boyfriends we then proceeded to demolish, but not unkindly). In the waiting line would be office-returnees and day laborers alike; his *bhel* and *sev puri* were magnificent, uniting people across all class lines. The *pani-puri*, round, spicy-sweet, exploding morsels with their questionable spiced-water filling, too sinful to resist, would be my final undoing. Many times I succumbed, along with the wall group, to the *pani-puri,* but I suffered later, inevitably cramping, throwing up, or otherwise ejecting the offending street food and its contaminated water into the night. Paps would then furiously round on me, "I am telling you not to go with those friends and eat on the road like that. Every time you do it and every time you vomit. When will you learn your lesson?" Weakly, I'd moan, "I'm not going to eat *bhel* ever again, promise!" And for that night, thinking queasily of the yellow and green bits that had floated in the toilet bowl, I meant it. Mum, because she could never leave anything alone, would keep on hectoring and admonishing well into the morning, "Naughty girl, you will spoil your insides. Then what will you do? End up in hospital only with cholera or typhoid." But it was always Paps who held my forehead as I threw up the multi-colored mess in the middle of the night, and Mum who continued to sleep.

Seema-Peema's father was a pilot for Air India. In the early years of our childhood, with India closed in so many ways to foreign presences or experiences, this was an occupation that was highly coveted, prestigious for father and children alike. When the Air India van, with its jaunty turbaned *maharaja* (now a pathetic joke as Air India's downward spiral continues) on the side carried uncle out of the gates of Sangeeta to the airport, the girls waved and preened a little from the wall. For me, each of their father's flights to London, Paris, or Singapore, which they announced nonchalantly, allowed me to dream a little of quiet streets, orderly lives, universities where I could debate and think without the dead weight of memorization and mugging, and of any escape from the sheltered, confining, and achingly familiar existence that I, in the inescapable irony that life always provides aplenty, now dream of longingly in my American life.

Their father's profession meant that they had a seemingly endless supply of all the most desirable things that catapulted one into the stratosphere of consumerism in socialist India: cheeses and shortbread biscuits from England, nuts and pistachios from Iran, thick chocolate triangles of Toblerone (which, when I tried them for the first time, I became hopelessly addicted to), Danish butter that we slathered on fresh hot-hot toasts ordered from the cook right off the grill for our tea, as well as jeans, t-shirts, and skirts in the latest styles that Indian girls at the time could only hope to take to their tailors to be replicated in poor-cousin fashion; although in my American life they would be coveted as "custom," these siblings had the real thing!

Of these, my oldest friends were ever and always generous. Never did they hide these goodies as many other Indian families might have, and did, in the grey steel *Godrej* cupboards (Parsi company, *baebee*!) known for their ability to withstand any assault. I even remember Mum secreting many a treasured box of dried fruits, cashews, and juicy sultanas given as Diwali gifts in the recesses of her *Godrej*, to be brought out and shared only in moderate amounts with our friends—we would surely have been slapped if we had frittered away goodies in an intemperate fashion. Never did Seema and Priya make a big deal of the unique good fortune of being the owners of heaps of this stuff, as many others might have, and did. I remember visiting yet another distant Aunty's house and being given English Cadbury's with a long introduction on how lucky we were to be eating these meltingly-creamy chocolates and how virtuous she was to be sharing her stock with us, but then she just had "*So* many friends from abroad!" And if Seema's and Priya's mother minded, she never showed it, taking the constant, daily, and surely annoying comings and goings to their terrace flat from all of us, and her girls' largesse in her stride.

Once, we were all on our way to Otter's Club at the edge of the sea in Bandra Bandstand with waves lapping at the rock walls along which we would sit and order sandwiches and hot *pakoras* after a swim, and where the wind would whip our hair into wild peaks and whirls. I mentioned that I absolutely hated my Indian swimsuit. It was the best that could be found—and that too with the utmost difficulty—at a small lingerie shop in Bandra which was crammed with stiff cotton brassieres and voluminous panties and overseen by a leering male attendant as lingerie shops inexplicably were. The swimsuit was a dreary, local affair with a drooping bottom and ill-fitting halter top in an ugly mustard yellow. Although a challenging color for many, for my sallow skin it was deadly. Yet, to go to Otters, so superior to our own Khar Gymkhana, even though Khar Gym had competition-standard tennis, badminton, cricket, and many other sports courts and facilities, as Mum was fond of pointing out that Otters didn't, I would have worn almost anything, even the sagging, yellow item. Seema later rummaged in her cupboard and brought out a sporty, spanking new navy blue Speedo with a blinding stripe that ran up and down the sides in slick rivers of white. "Here. Just take this; neither of us has ever worn it, and besides we have others now." I demurred repeatedly, but when aunty nodded her assent, I took the present and wore it to Otters—and everywhere a swimsuit was required.

That remained my swimsuit until it became too small to cram into. Paps put an end to it by ordering me to get a new one from a local shop or to stop swimming, *khalaas*. "It looks so bad, what will everyone think?" (Aunties? Cousins? The general population? Who did he mean? It didn't matter). "Go change immediately." Paps was the keeper of our appearances, looking with a regular and critical eye for signs of excess—too much makeup, too-short skirts, or too-tight jeans. Then Rashna would obediently change because she hated conflict, but I would fly at him. "I'm not changing! You always spoil everything. I hate you!" But because a cross word from him would make me dissolve into tears, the squabbles always ruined my evening or night out. There was many a party where I would moodily relive what he had said, while relentlessly bad disco music blared, "Superfreak, superfreak, she's super freaky," and boys and girls, sweat dripping from brows in the sweltering Bombay heat, gyrated energetically, stopped for cold-drink, beer, and *samosa* breaks, and believed themselves to be in America.

Ours was the last generation where the music—always disco and pop for our "dance parties"—was imported from abroad. Someone, or someone's cousin or friend, visiting from the U.S. or U.K. would bring down cassettes of Michael Jackson, George Michael, Donna Summer, The Bee Gees, Blondie and, of course, ABBA. Inevitably, the music was several months or even years late. Surely, American youth listening in on our parties would have been amused at the enthusiasm with which we were still making the dance moves to "Love to Love You Baby," when they had long since progressed to Madonna or the Boss. But if they had seen Ganesh break dancing to "Billie Jean" with supreme expertise, they would have been impressed, so finely had he perfected the steps and so unselfconsciously did he execute the twirls and thrusts to our combined exhortations, encouragement, and laughter that was more with him than at him.

Those who presumed themselves to be the more knowledgeable and cooler among us, or those with some deeper familial link to America, would listen to classic rock: The Who, The Doors, The Stones, Pink Floyd, thrilling bands that evoked wildly forbidden things like drugs, defiance, and freedom. Many a night I remember being crammed into a small, ancient, seatbelt-less Fiat (Arjun's? Arun's?), which could in reality barely hold four but often had to contain seven or eight of us, making our sputtering way down Carter Road's sultry seafront, rocking to "Lay Down Sally" and feeling infinitely superior to the other cars cruising up and down the road leaving trails of pure disco or high pitched Hindi film songs dying in their wake. Today, Mumbaikars, exporting their own music to the West—Bollywood fusion, Hinglish pop, Bhangra rock, Hindi rap— are confident leaders of a global youth culture where we were followers and yearners, hemmed in by the reality of India's enforced cultural and economic borders, but liberated perhaps by our yearning and striving for more than we had.

Negotiating permission for a party with Paps was an ordeal that left me exhausted and embittered. "Be back home by midnight," he would say, insanely. It was already ten o'clock, I hadn't even been picked up yet and the party would surely not begin before eleven at the earliest. Hiding my strapless top under a jacket that I would later remove in the car, I would step up and challenge his irrationality. "That's so stupid, nothing starts before eleven," I would shout. "Midnight, of course that's right, everything ends at twelve," he would reiterate stubbornly. And then, as if he were being supremely reasonable, "Okay *baba*, be home by twelve-thirty then." Mum would then step in, propelled by vicarious images of youth and fun, twin inciters that she succumbed to and defended repeatedly. "Let her go, Bomi, let her have fun." Then she and he would bicker, he to blame her for neglect and dereliction of duty, and she to respond tartly about his repressiveness and orthodoxy. Somewhere in between, I would slip out for my party, drooping a little, but cheering up significantly when some new boys from town (St. Mary's, really? Campion?), or my Bombay Scottish crushes, or later the Engineer, the one who would be my first and last real boyfriend in India, were spotted in the crush of friends, acquaintances, hangers-on, worthless *lookhas*, aspirants, minor starlets, major stars (this was Bandra, home to half of Bollywood, after all) and friends of friends of friends.

When I returned, so well past midnight that it would have been useless to explain or excuse away, Paps was always lurking in the shadows of the veranda, his ear attuned to my key in the door. "Lock the door and go to sleep," he would say resignedly. Now that I was home, his fight was all spent, to be re-gathered for another day. Creeping into my bed, I could hear Rashna snore softly. Her life always seemed easier than mine: less yearning, less conflict, more acceptance, and therefore more peace. But in those days, since we didn't talk much and certainly didn't share heart-felt talk, *dil ni vat* as Firdaushad mockingly labeled such talk, I did not know much about her. Today, not a day goes by when I don't call Rashna in her frosty New England abode. It's as if she were in her wooden four-poster bed beside mine, both with the tops inexplicably sawed off, in our old bedroom in West Breeze. Her voice always answers and we pick up where we left off the day before, and sometimes the conversations only last for two minutes, but we still manage to say everything.

As the whirring fan above desultorily moved around warm and moisture heavy Bombay air, and in the distance a gentle roar of cars on Linking Road signaled that it was past the two hour window between 2 and 4 am when Bombay really did seem to sleep and relative silence reigned, I would relive the night, feel my familiar pangs of dissatisfaction, incompleteness, and diffused longing to be somewhere else, have something else, do something else, and finally fall asleep.

Chapter 7

PUTLI

In the Khalakdina Terrace flat, three big bedrooms stood side-by-side, adjacent to the vast living-dining room, *tabelas* of my father's design nightmares. Each one had doors opening in the front and back to vast corridors, the front of each also holding a wide window whose wooden shutters were usually thrown open to the sun-soaked front corridor and thence to the windows that lined the front of the flat and opened out onto the road. Each bedroom had en suite bathrooms, massive, old, stone affairs that some modern designer would have itched to remodel ("So much space!"). One of those rooms, almost a small flat in itself, was Mamina's, with her familiar dressing table, mirrors, baubles, and two comfortable four-poster beds on which we slumbered and read in the afternoons. Another was Kayzad's family's, with more modern, mid-century furniture rather than the old Parsi pieces, and with other updates—built-ins to hold record and cassette players, books, and curios that Nilufer Aunty had carefully collected from her trips to Singapore, Hong Kong, England, or Switzerland, and of which she was inordinately proud. The other bedroom, the middle one, always seemed shut up and often had a padlock on the outside of the front-facing door, one of those palm-sized, indestructible Godrej *talas* that Indians so favored and trusted as the last word on security. Inside lived, incredibly, for it was in their own home, a woman whom no one seemed to know much about.

Rashna and I had only ever seen her small, squat, dark-clothed silhouette turning a fat key in the padlock and hurrying out of the front door into the dusk with her head bent and covered with a *mathoobanoo*, a type of scarf favored by only the most traditional of Parsi women. Certainly no aunty of mine ever wore a *mathoobanoo* except to the Agiary, where all heads required cover, whether via *sari pallu*, colorful silken headscarves, or red velveteen *topis*. When she was in the flat, she never seemed to need to step into the remainder of the house, seemingly using her room as a separate abode unconnected to the rest of us. She seemed very old to us, but in actuality was probably around seventy; her silence and hurry, dark garb, lowered gaze, and mysterious presence led her to be eventually labeled a witch and magician by the incorrigible Kayzad. When she emerged from the room where the window shutters were always drawn and the doors always closed and locked so that we had no idea what lay inside, Kayzad often gave pursuit, pulling at her *mathoobanoo*, beseeching her to say something, shouting in her wake, "Putli, Putli, you old *batli*!" (nonsensically, bottle) until she escaped, hissing, out of the front door and Rashna and I rocked backwards, too afraid, unwilling, and ashamed to anger her.

Mum was not able to shed much light on Putli. We knew that she was a relative of my grandfather's and that she had no one else left and nowhere else left to go to, and that Grandpa had promised that she would always have a home in his house. This was enough for the permanent presence of someone who might as well have been a stranger; relatives took care of their own and *khandaani* promises like that had to be kept. And so, Putli had a home at Khalakdina Terrace. But of course, we were all aware that this was not one's traditional joint-family set-up, where the extended family members may not always get along with each other but at least always interacted in the shared physical space and at least were called Aunty or Uncle by the kids whom they spoilt even if the adults were at logger-heads. To refer to an old woman who was not a beloved and familiar household member, as Roda (or affectionately, Rodi) was, by a diminutive of her first name, as Kayzad did, was inconceivably rude and spoke volumes about Putli's station in our lives. Mum, Roda, and Mamina referred to her as Putla, that more substantial name ending conveying a semblance of the respect that her ripe age demanded, but we kids were only rarely urged to say Putla Aunty, and Kayzad ran wild with shouts of "Putli!" ringing through the house.

Where Putli ate (for she didn't share the old stone kitchen quarters with its two sets of cooks holding domain for Mamina and Nilufer Aunty within), where she went, why she stayed in locked and stifling darkness without the freeing light of sunshine ever let in, how she passed her time behind the shut doors and windows, why she shunned the familiarity and comfort of the others who lived in the same flat, I asked and asked but never got answers to; nobody seemed to know. But running past her middle room on the front corridor, I always cast a quick and wary eye for evidence of Putli's whereabouts. If the padlock was on, she was gone—again—and I could breathe more easily. If it wasn't, I wondered if she might leave a door ajar, and we would get to peek in as I sometimes had, seeing shadows of old, solid furniture crowded within, or best of all (worst of all?), we might see Putli herself, dark-clad, round, sack-like and bewhiskered, avoiding us, hurrying outside, and leaving Kayzad's hectoring calls dying in her wake.

Over the years, I realized that Putli did speak to us, a few spare words to Rashna and me, once extending a gnarled hand over my hair outside her room and disappearing inside as Kayzad came flying up. Perhaps she found our silence agreeable, our smallness unthreatening, our weekly appearances at Khalakdina without fault and without a past. Perhaps our presence as weekly guests echoed her transience in the flat, or she sensed our fear of her and sought to reassure.

When I celebrated my eighth birthday at Mamina's, my grandmother did the traditional *sagan* that evening. A newly made birthday dress from our tailor, a Dutch chocolate truffle cake, (never buttercream icing, that ubiquitous adornment to all my sons' American birthday parties), and crunchy potato wafers. Step up, extend my neck for the garland with the favored flowers of fresh jasmine and fluffy yellow marigold sewn together; red good-luck *tilla* placed carefully (carelessly if it was Mum, which was why she was never allowed to paint the *tillas* on us) on my forehead from the rounded edge of Mamina's thumb. After rice was scattered on me from the large silver salver holding the *sagan-ni-sais*—heavy, ceremonial, carved silver receptacles for the garland, *tilla,* and a long-necked sprinkler for rosewater—we saw to our surprise, that Putli, hurrying down the corridor as usual to the front door, detoured right into the living room and pressed a white envelope into my hand.

Because you could never open presents or *pareekas* (white envelopes holding gift money for birthdays, *navjotes*, and weddings, sometimes with a blood-red *sagan-no-tillo* embellishing the front where they were addressed in carefully executed handwriting, in bold red ink for luck) until after all the guests had gone and only in the privacy of your home, I didn't think to open the curiously fat packet until we were back home in Santacruz. But once I bounded upstairs, gifts were unwrapped, paper tossed, and *pareekas* opened with my usual internal guilt conversation with myself about whether I would keep all the gift money, which I felt I had done nothing to deserve, or turn it in to my parents. More and more it pained me to take anything from them, even though both kept the keys forever dangling in the locks of their twin wooden cupboards in their bedroom, and we were instructed to take whatever we needed out of their drawers, no questions asked, for *golas* and sweeties and shoes and hairbands—"Just take the money, dahling, from my drawer, take, take." Giving them some of my birthday money, I felt, would at least help balance the equation, cement my sometimes shaky status as a good daughter, and be a miniscule way towards somehow repaying them.

From Putli's packet, which I ripped with abandon, fell a shining oval bracelet with a thud onto our polished, multi-colored, hexagonal tiled floor. Mum gasped and picked it up, speechless for once. I was less interested at first, for it was not immediately beautiful, but rather a bracelet of two thick dull-gold wires within which were set thirteen large, winking, round, yellow diamonds and a gold clasp which opened in the back so that it could be slid onto the wrist. Later, needless to say, despite all the sets of diamond-ruby and diamond-emerald art deco and filigree and Parsi-Victorian baubles that we had learned to take in with practiced and unimpressed eyes, this bracelet held us in thrall, so big were the curiously yellow diamonds, so insanely big, all thirteen of them many karats each.

The next morning, I learned that Putli had died that night. She had been found on the busy road at the back of Khalakdina Terrace, dead of a heart attack outside a lowly tea-shop with its open shop-front with flies dancing around heaps of *samosas* and *pakoras* and big *kadais* of frying oil and nauseating wafts of crude spices. Is this where she had dined day after day in humiliation, with the *shopwalla* looking on as she furtively ate the greasy *wada-pao* or *pao bhaji*, unthinkable for the rest of us? Or perhaps she had *preferred* this, the uncomplicated honesty of paying for what one bought and ate, there and then, no favors, no gratitude, no payback, no conversation, in a city which freely allowed such independence, but only for some women.

My mother and aunts discussed her death and her gift to me, and the coincidence of timing did not go unnoticed. In fact, in India nothing was considered coincidental or random, but rather the result of a quietly-gathered unseen plan, some karmic force or other that rewarded or repaid or punished. My aunts chattered and speculated as to what had made Putli do such an uncharacteristic thing, and that too just before she was to die. It was definitely an omen, they agreed, but whether auspicious or inauspicious was as yet unclear. Eventually, Mummy put an end to the musings by condemning them as old wives tales.

After some weeks, the middle room at Khalakdina Terrace was finally opened to reveal more black-lacquer Parsi-Raj furniture in piles and groups that Nilufer Aunty brought out and had polished and displayed as some of the ground floor flat's handsomest pieces—tallboys and occasional tables and show-cases. Curiously, her room had held the most striking of the family furniture, (carefully chosen by my grandparents for their unusual house-guest, perhaps to underscore the welcome?) well preserved by their lack of use and protection from any light.

Later, it became Kayzad's room and we were startled to see one day that after a trip to Europe, where Nilufer Aunty had been introduced to a new kind of modern art, she had hung a large portrait of a naked woman done in the mixed-media style of that time, with critical body parts realistically, or unrealistically, curving out of the frame. Other favorites in this multidimensional style were, I remember, landscapes with dogs and horses with flowing, 3-D manes. She said this was the height of envelope pushing and edginess, all the rage in Europe, but Rashna and I thought it was the most embarrassing spectacle we had the misfortune to be stuck in the middle of. Kayzad, of course, was characteristically (and for us, impossibly) nonchalant and unconcerned at the *tamasha* being unleashed in his own room.

Much later, Gool had daringly worn the bracelet at my wedding reception at the Taj Lands End after a familiar debate. On the one hand, if these pieces of *khandaani* jewelry, handed down from generations past and kept in steel bank safe-deposit boxes were never worn, what was the use? One's life would be over soon anyway, and one would never enjoy the beautiful jewels; on the other hand, if a piece was lost or stolen, how to forgive oneself? Some people lacked the courage to ever wear their heirloom jewelry and instead came to the weddings and *navjotes* in rich and gorgeously-embroidered *garas*, those exquisite hand-threaded saris with elaborate Chinese and Chinese-inspired embroidery of trees, birds, and flowers in brilliant colors, with costume jewelry in their ears and around their necks and wrists. The rationale was that although a robber could snatch away the precious jewelry, no one was ever likely to tear the priceless *garas* off anybody's person.

Gool wrestled with herself and was finally convinced that the bracelet was fitting for the momentous occasion of her first-born's wedding reception to the American, and certainly Rashna and I encouraged her, idly, not caring one way or another—"Wear it, Mummy, wear it, everyone will be amazed!" And then, when it was lost or stolen in the partying and the ensuing melee at the hotel, Gool spiraled into the first and only breakdown that I had ever seen her in, moping and taking to her bed like a sick woman for eight whole days while Rashna and I commiserated, consoled, and finally told her exasperatedly to snap out of it, that it was ridiculous to carry on like this over an inanimate object, and that it was enough already. But deep within ourselves, Rashna and I understood that it wasn't the bracelet itself, but its impossible beauty, the families that had held it and cherished it, and the magnificent eras that it had seen, now long gone, finished, *khalaas*, along with their people, their relatives, along with Parsis themselves. Neither we, nor anyone we knew, would ever again be able to afford anything like it in any of our lifetimes, and we were filled with pity for our poor mother.

As to why I had been given it, and how Putli had come to have it, and the old questions of what she was all about and how her life had been—it was now too late for answers. I wish that we had sought them then, that I had had the courage to reach out to her and let her know that I cared about who she was and where she went when she vanished from the apartment for hours on end. I wish that I had mentioned to her that perhaps she could have stopped in the living room in Khalakdina and had tea with us and it would have been alright even if awkward, and that she needn't have always hurried out of the front door as if she couldn't bear to be in the same house. I never said those things, of course, because children in those days didn't say those kinds of things in an adult world, and perhaps also because I selfishly felt that it didn't really matter because I didn't need another aunty, I had them aplenty as it was. But it seems that she already knew what I sought to ask, because one day, she had given me that dazzling bracelet, just like that, in a modicum of response.

Image 1 | My family on the day of my *novjote*.

Image 2 | My maternal great grand-parents. My grandma, Coomie, is in the middle with her three brothers by her side. Her sister Roda, the baby, is with my great grandmother.

Image 3 | My parents, Gool and Bomi, on the terrace of West Breeze in their first year of marriage.

Image 4 | My parents during their wedding ceremony, facing the *dasturs* and flanked by relatives.

Image 5 | My mother on her wedding morning at a pre-wedding ceremony. She is flanked by some of my aunts, including, on her right, Silloo Aunty.

Image 6 | My father, Bomi, with me in his arms.

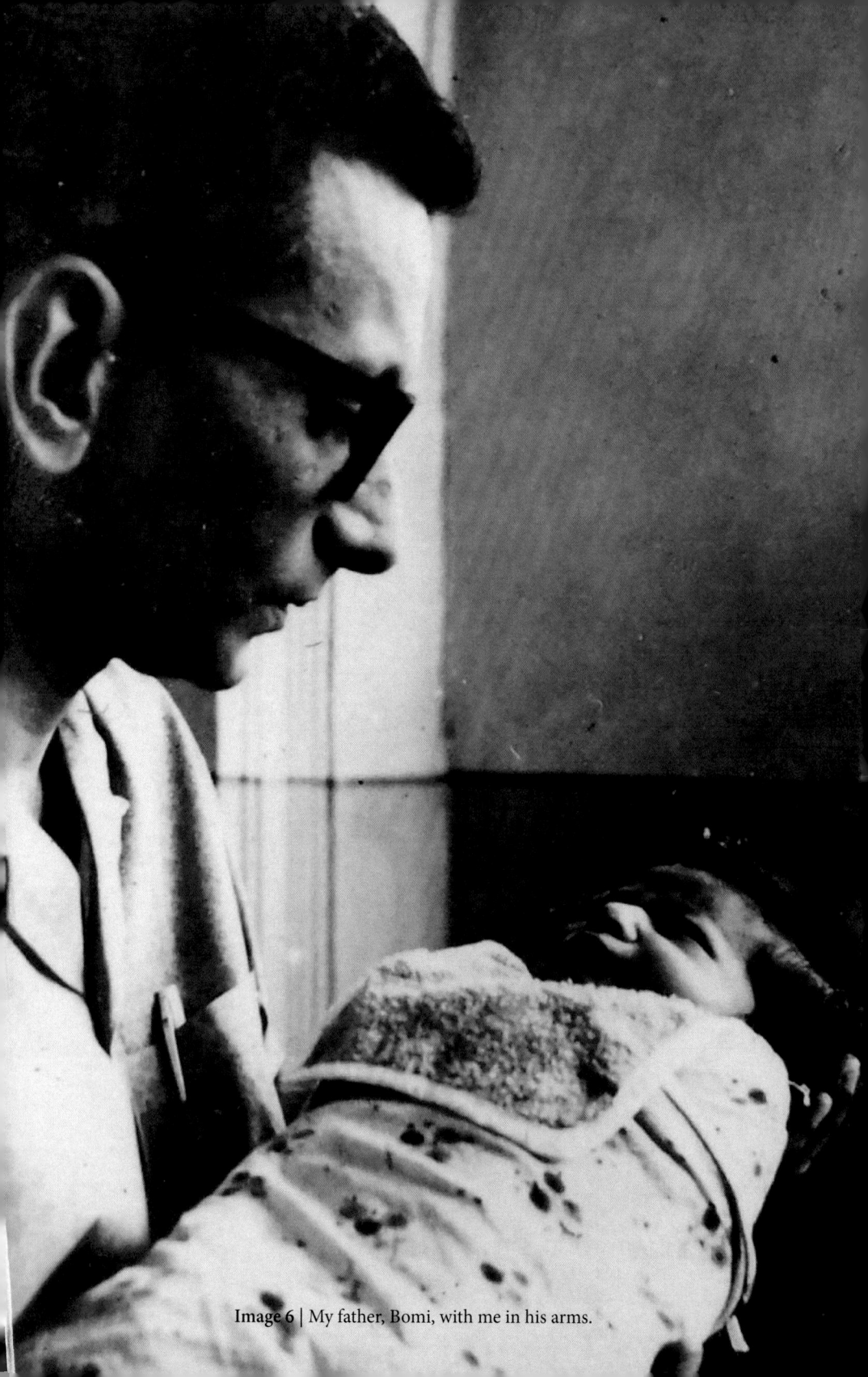

Image 7 | My mother with me in her arms.

Image 8 | My mother, Gool, and myself.

Image 9 | My grandmother, Coomie.

Image 10 | West Breeze and Sea Breeze bungalows during their construction in 1930.

Image 11 | With my mother on my birthday with the celebratory *tillo* on my forehead and flower garland.

Image 12 | My sister and I at my *navjote* ceremony.

Image 14 | My mother, Roda Aunty, and I with my younger son at West Breeze.

Chapter 8

SCHOOL AT MAHIM BAY

In the morning, every morning, we saw a familiar tussle. As Mum bustled around getting ready for her job teaching Geography, a great love of her life, Rashna and I would get ready for another school day. Our grey Bombay Scottish uniforms were carefully laid out along with clean white blouses. The durable grey pinafore would be worn twice before washing, blue sash tied and retied so that it was not too high (gauche) or too low (lest it come under the eagle eye of a sharp-tongued teacher for being too suggestive, although many a girl tried), and the blue tie knotted into place. Then, we would quickly gobble down the half-boiled egg so favored by Paps, which we would later rebel against and reject forever. Indeed I don't know how I managed to swallow its soft, slithering, undercooked-ness for so many years, but in my mind I hear Mum, urging loudly and pressing its health benefits and Paps, noisily dousing it with salt and pepper and mixing it with relish.

Then the grabbing of water bottles (later rejected as uncool: "not hep, *yaar*!"), lunches taken from an impatient Mary Lunjen, and the wait for Paps to finish his careful dressing and drive us to school. "Come on, hurry up, you always make us late. We'll have to wait outside the entrance gate and everyone will know we were late when they go past for Assembly!" we would screech. But Paps would maddeningly insist that there was "plenty of time," and even that we would "be early, very early, just wait and see." Then he would unhurriedly emerge wearing a carefully put-together suit and tie in the early days, then later the bush shirt-trouser combination many Indians preferred as the memories of colonial times receded ever further, and even later a quick foray into the half-sleeved, two-piece safari suit in adventurous pastel colors, some of which would arrive fully-tailored ("custom!") from Hong Kong. This last ensemble I was glad he rejected quickly because its effect was slightly vulgar to our eyes and flashily Hindi-filmish, and we girls eventually badgered him into abandoning it forever.

At the first bus stop on Linking Road, we would scan the waiting figures spilling out onto the road, searching for Sorab or other relatives from Sea Breeze; Anahita and Arnavaz, who would be all dressed up, lipstick-rouged, ready and waiting for the bus to take them to their work in town (I much envied them, for I would rather have been dressed up and going into my beloved town-side than to another unforgiving day at school), or Miss Race, our History teacher who lived in the area—much to my dismay—and most certainly expected us to stop if she was waiting. Paps was most delighted when Miss Race was found among the surging crowd. Impeccably dressed in beautifully coordinated skirts and blouses or tailored dresses with matching heels, purse, and made-up face, I had to admit that the acerbic Miss Race hid the heavy and scathing sarcasm she used at school very well indeed and even simpered a little for Paps. "Thank you so much, Mr. Pavri," she would gush, "These buses are so useless. Two came and went without stopping-only, and when the next one comes, everyone will rush in like hooligans!" "Hooligans" was a favored word of many Bombay Scottish teachers, especially to describe us students. "Ruffians" was another, and "loafers" yet another. These words describing societal undesirables I rarely hear now, but they fill me with a delighted nostalgia for the outraged images of teachers and aunties past.

Paps and Miss Race would proceed to make robust conversation, uncharacteristic for the quietly-inclined Bomi, while Rashna and I wouldn't manage a word, except for a weak and gulping "Good morning, Miss" when she charmingly and falsely greeted us. The old Fiat would make its laborious crawl through the morning traffic through Bandra, then the fish-odorous Mahim Causeway, and then up to Cadell Road and school itself as we anxiously prayed for an on-time arrival, for the car not to break down, or to run out of water, or some other indignity that had occurred on so many previous drives. Later, Paps would wax eloquent about Miss Race and make up one of his nonsense rhymes in her honor, while we would shriek in horror:

Miss Race, Miss Race
All dressed up in lace
We notice with grace
The bloom on your face

The three grey peaks of Scottish looking stoically out to sea would come into view and Paps would deposit us at the gates (Lucky Paps, he to drive fully into town, we to stay behind!). We would plead for the gate to be opened and rush past the *gurkha* in a desperate sprint to the classroom to deposit our bags, while Miss Race coolly walked in, the crusty *gurkha* opening the gate wide for her and even bestowing on her a toothy smile. If the long line of students was already snaking its way to Assembly Hall, we would abandon our bags in a safe haven along the way and try our best to blend in, hearts pounding for fear of being caught and asked to wait outside the assembly with other tardy arrivals for reprisals later. Teachers monitored our deportment, kept us moving, and checked uniforms for neatness and length as we tried to make our way unseen to be next to best friends or to better vantage spots to gossip by and view the boys lining up beside. Inside Assembly Hall, Miss Pinto was banging harder than usual on the piano as the hapless class responsible for leading the hymn for the morning withered under her fiery temper and screams, "Stupid children, are you deaf? Can't hear the notes I'm playing and playing? Start from the beginning. Again! Repeat!" But she was magnificent in her fury and in the beautiful sound she was invariably able to bring out of us.

Then Principal Mathews made his ponderous way to the stage, thin lips tightly pinched inwards, his face registering his usual distaste for one and all, any and everything. A hush descended as he pompously declared, "Good morning," and waited for our inevitable sing-song, "Good mooooor-ning, Sir Math-eeeeews!" Sometimes, we would have to repeat the greeting over and over until we got it just right and without any whiff of impertinence. Staccato-style, we would finally shout in unison, "Good mor-ning-sir-math-ews," and it was finally accepted. Then came my favorite part, the hymn. If I was lucky that day, it would be of my treasured ones out of an embarrassment of riches: "Abide with Me" (rumored to have been one of Mahatma Gandhi's favorites), "Rock of Ages," "The Lord's My Shepherd," "Guide me O Thou Great Jehovah," or, if we were poised before an oncoming break, the promise of "God Be With You Till We Meet Again." The great hall filled with voices beautiful and awful, but palpable always was the thing Mum had explained to me before: in those moments I had no doubt that all, or at least most, of our minds, whether Christian, Muslim, Hindu, Sikh, or Parsi, were on decidedly higher things.

These indescribably beautiful hymns I thought surely all had forgotten but I was pleasantly surprised when childhood Scottishites met recently and waxed heavily nostalgic. In my American life, I encounter these age-old hymns sometimes, but their tunes have been modernized, jazzified, Americanized and, for me, mangled beyond recognition. But on the great wide webway I can search and find the original versions, and sometimes Scottishites write in their blogs and posts about what these hymns meant to them and how they could never forget them, and I think of all of us, Indian kids raised in different religions or no religion united by the sublime sound and what it invoked—that sense of something greater, more powerful, our better selves.

That feeling of intense wonder and longing for an unknown yet still knowable truth that the hymns brought in their wake, remains to be found in other things as my life has unfolded: a stolen glance at my boys as they sleep, the Max Bruch violin concerto which surely soars beyond mere human composition, my beautiful boy playing soccer with long, spindly, joyful legs, or re-reading the profound and affecting end of Styron's *Sophie's Choice* about the beauteous but damned Sophie, a promise of morning eventually and always breaking no matter how bleak the day before, a "morning, excellent and fair."

This, I think, is what Plato meant when he wrote about "the Good," the enlightenment "beyond truth and knowledge," that we could all attain with the right wisdom. In my American classroom, the students and I struggle to name what this could be, what he meant. It's this moment of pure acknowledgment, insight, beauty, and, I think, each of us could have these moments through different impetuses, differing knowledge. Plato, of course, discounted feeling for thinking. He talked about *knowing* "the Good" through deep and long study. But "the Good" necessarily evokes feeling, even though Plato might have denied it, downgrading as he did emotion and sentiment. As he averred, "the Good" is indeed provoked by a knowledge, a highest comprehending, but what it then brings out in us, I believe, is a pure and grateful flood of *feeling* that we can reach such an awe-inspiring and ultimate understanding. For that moment, we seem to have the answers to those pesky and eternal existential questions of what life is about.

The hymns, embedded in their beautiful original music from centuries ago which Miss Pinto faithfully followed, albeit with some rather unfeeling pounding of the keys, started each of our days with this moment of reflection, a struggle for understanding and acceptance of things greater than ourselves. All through the school years however, we never discussed the hymns. Strange that something that started every day of our lives we took for granted, never elevated to importance, never even admitted, until much later, that we loved to sing them and that they had suffused our lives with beauty and wisdom.

Principal Mathews would then make some key announcements, cautions, and round off Assembly with the inevitable "Our Father" prayer, which each student comfortably interpreted in line with their own faith. It seemed so simple then; we never suspected religious motives, we accepted differences easily, we simply took the beauty and read into it what we wanted, we never dwelt on fundamentalist dogma, and we never thought God only belonged to some. India was more truly secular in practice then, even while religion was, of course, still supremely important in a deeply religious country. As children we didn't dwell on religious differences, accepting them as part of life in our city, and terrorism and pogroms were not within the realm of our knowing. Later, Mumbai would become familiar with both those imposters, with cycles of reeling and rallying from bomb blasts redefining the new city as it confronted its own problems and mirrored what was occurring in the world.

On other days, when culprits had been caught in some prank or unacceptable exuberance—Rahul , Vijay, Dominic, Aziz, always the same handful of offenders—Principal Mathews would casually announce a caning, and a shrinking boy (later toughened into acquiring a careful veneer of indifference) would step up or be pulled up to receive the whipping. As they cried out despite their best efforts at stoicism, my heart filled with childish heartbreak, my stomach tense even after the boy in question was back in class and laughing. I could never understand why we didn't revolt against the routine and habitual caning that went on not just in our school but in every Bombay school, and just make it stop. Immediately. *Bus.* But we bore many things in our stride in those days, accepting, although with growing questions, age-old practices as necessary and evidence of how things should be. And indeed the receivers of the caning, if they are to be believed, assure us today that they were singularly unaffected.

Bombay Scottish was built by Scottish missionaries in 1859, "Scotsmen true in days gone by, all honor is their right" as our school song went. It was first an orphanage, then a school for the British, and then of course for all of us Indians. Here Mummy had gone, her classmates including movie royal Shashi Kapoor (whom we met years later on a plane from Goa and suffered teenage humiliation by Mum's accosting of and reminiscing with the actor although the two Scottishites seemed to have much to talk about), a host of Anglo-Indians (the last of them before their mass exodus out of India), and middle-class Indian boys and girls from every community and religion who would develop into the foundation of post-independence Bombay. In her time it was a ten-minute drive from Palamkot Hall, her temporary abode with Roda Aunty in the heart of Dadar Parsi Colony. In my time it was a tense fifteen minutes from Santacruz with Paps. Today, traffic all over Mumbai is gridlocked and unpredictable and it could take an hour or more.

Principal Mathews ran the school like an army garrison. The grounds, including the original structure which housed his family upstairs and a small hall with lustrous carved wooden mantles downstairs, had grown to include two new wings with new buildings and classrooms—and all were immaculately maintained. In the back a vast and outspread Banyan provided a place for many an impromptu lunch and chatter ("under the spreading Banyan tree!") and fields beyond invited games during breaks and Physical Training (PT) classes. Around these fields tall buildings sprang up as the years progressed, and I thought about the lives just beyond their windows, as open kitchens wafted down lunchtime smells of *dals* boiling and rice steaming. How normal and everyday their life seemed and how much more preferable than the burden of always, always doing well at school! Games and sports were never my thing, and I eyed them warily before inevitably turning back to the well-loved buildings, to special spots outside classrooms and in long corridors, seeking recourse in the original heritage structures, wondrous old offices and classrooms that smelt of another era.

The Mathews family quarters I had seen once or twice were breathtaking—wood plank floors rarely seen in Bombay, where cool stone or marble tiles ruled, shining walnut paneling, high ceilings and rows of windows that opened across the school to the calm, grey sea beyond. The small beach in front of the bay was one of those rarest of Bombay sights: an area of almost complete desolation which, perhaps because of the school's watchful eye, the hoards of the city's masses fighting for an open stretch—had not found, had not set up food stalls around, had not made into makeshift bedrooms and bathrooms and *matka* joints or open-air gambling dens fueled by home-made hooch. Once, when we had bunked class to run across, all we saw was open sea, sandy, tree-filled beach, and only one or two *mawalees*, the local ruffians who were the bane of our teachers' existences. They came up leeringly but were quelled by Neera's acid tongue and they slunk off, not knowing whether to laugh at her hilarious and cutting remarks or protest their insulted manhood.

In Bombay Scottish, I navigated growing up, accepting the totality of who I was and what I loved and wanted. I would never be a winner at Sports Day no matter how much Gool willed it (she had since turned her sights on Rashna, even dressing her up as a boy for the first four years of her life in hopes of creating a sports-loving tomboy), I would always be bookish, I would revel in the friendships and lightness and froth but carefully hold myself at the edges of things. Outside, looking in, was the place of my choice and the spot that offered me greatest comfort: the double-consciousness of W.E.B. Du Bois, a tacit understanding of difference among similars, but for me acquired at will, which of course was not quite what Du Bois had meant. Above all, my eyes even then were trained on something else, a something which slowly but surely shaped into searching, finding, understanding, and eventually, leaving.

Being at school in Bombay in the seventies and eighties was not an easy thing. Marks mattered above all and without a first class you could never hope to get into the best colleges and never anywhere in the Sciences stream (thankfully I had my eyes trained on the Social Sciences). Children were intensely competitive, teachers were scathing, boys were caned, and all were humiliated with equal and easy regularity. At night, I dreamt of trying to do math problems and being unable, the problems not making any sense, and repeatedly failing the complicated exams made up of nonsense numbers. I would shake myself awake, terrified, reminding myself that things weren't that bad, that I may never be the brilliant mathematician, but I was always of the good mind—Vohu Mano. In our Zoroastrian prayers, reason, morality, and learning—the good mind—were elevated. Similarly, the ancient Greeks, who would come after the Persians of the Zoroastrian era, conquer their lands, and benefit from the philosophical groundwork already laid, also emphasized these values. When I teach Greek philosophy, I hear many echoes of my own ancient religion that today hardly anyone knows about, and those who do know believe it long dead.

The fear of failure remained. But there was also laughter, much ribbing of unseasoned teachers, confident kids challenging a hapless new History teacher to a duel about the significance of the Indus Valley civilization—and winning. And the excitement of boys that we were in love with for that month or week—the secret knowledge rarely shared and that even best friends would only know if they followed our eyes at just the right moments, romances that would never be acted upon but watched from the outside and enacted furtively in our heads. And teachers we feared or loved, and sometimes both: Miss Da Silva, the vice principal, in her impeccable floral dresses and flair-filled hats and matching low-heeled pumps, vast-chested, imperious, but kind; Sir Rodricks, long-haired, dreamy, and lost in his art room among scattered canvases and brushes while the boys threw paint at the girls and the real artists among us (the slow-moving Divya, who was also the best student in class and came first every year without fail, and the out-spoken Neera, whose depictions of village belles with flashy jewels and curvy bodies Sir Rodricks loved, and were also precursors to a talented fashion designer in the making) begged them to stop; Miss Bose, young, dashing, short-skirted, small wire glasses slipping down her long, thin nose, long brown hair flicked to one side and another, so enthralled with the Indian History she taught and in turn, enthralling many of the girls and (especially) boys in the school; Miss Kingdom, soprano par excellence, whose clear, soaring voice made even the cultural heathens among us stop and listen and who later married a German and emigrated to sing abroad because there was no funding for the arts in those last pre-global decades.

There were small heartbreaks: when Rahul Silvestre, he of the Italian father and Tamilian mother, rakish, boisterous, warm-hearted tease, long-striding Sports Day hero, failed sixth standard and had to repeat the class—and once again do the same in the ninth standard. I think Rahul was just fine—even teachers exasperated by his lack of enthusiasm for studies still loved the boy, couldn't help but warm to his endless effervescence, and would take care of him, and there were many boys and girls who still worshiped him. But I wept silently into my pillow at the injustice of his penalty, my heart aching because I thought his must surely be too. On Facebook recently, news spread like wildfire of Rahul's untimely death. All the girls wrote about their sweet boy, their secret (and now public) crush. But, like one more Rahul-imprinted stunt (although it certainly did not originate from him), the joke was on them; he was alive and well and somewhere in Italy or a provincial Northern Indian city—somewhere, anyway, most unlikely for a supremely Bombay boy to surface in. If he could have seen the posts, he would surely have laughed. I noticed later that some of these posts were quietly deleted by no-doubt red-faced girls (now women) sitting at their computers in different corners of the world, while others lingered like flowers thrown in the memory of this larger-than-life class-mate who refused to engage in the Indian game of "mugging" at every waking hour, to follow it up with tuitions in Math and Science, to suffer silently on the all-important altar of marks and grades. He was not one to butter up teachers and adhere strictly to prevailing norms, but rather one who forged his own path and repeated classes with insouciance and learnt not to care so much and no doubt made his mark on the fledgling Bombay DJ industry and wherever else he is rumored to have turned up, and on all of us in exactly his own way.

Chapter 9

Weekends at Khandala

Over the next half-century after Paps's graduation, his friends from the J.J. School of Arts ("founded by a Parsi, Tinaz-*dikra*!") formed a tight-knit group that became our closest family friends. Quickly moving into places of prominence in the art and architecture world of Bombay, these friends and other peers had great career success. In fact, if you look at the Indian Institute of Architects' (AII) Hall of Fame honorees for 2012, it is a veritable who's who of Paps's colleagues and friends; household (at least in our household!) names like Pheroze Kudianwala, Atul Desai, Raja Adaeri, and our own Rusi Khambatta, who became the President of the AII and traveled the world lecturing on town planning, architecture, and the Indian city and is still, in his eighties, highly sought-after and magically as dynamic and dapper as ever. Another friend, DM, designed hotels and some of the most famous of Bombay's residences, including Il Palazzo where he lived in his 13th floor paradise from where we could look out to the shining arc of the Queen's Necklace. And Paps, quiet, independent, uncompromised (on the outside, looking in?), remained one of their most treasured friends.

This was a glamorous group to our young eyes. There was DM, who had met and married the young German girl, Uschi, in England after the war, bringing her home to Bombay and ensconcing her on that high-up floor of Il Palazzo with the balcony overlooking the Queen's Necklace and rooms full of paintings by then up-and-coming Indian artists like Gaitonde and Hussain. There were the Camas, dashing and full of energy, their weeks full of parties and events to which they faithfully dragged Mum and Paps, their Dadar home full of laughter, its old Parsi Colony exterior of a somber, stone symmetry belying the modern, bold colors they favored inside, which they completely remodeled with verve and abandon every two years. These irrepressible Camas seemed to know the most unlikely and most impressive of people—Queen's Freddie Mercury's (Farrokh

Balsara's) parents owned the flat above theirs in their Parsi Colony building, and when visiting Bombay, spoke freely of their son who was idolized by all my friends. There were also the Bondes, with the loud and raucous Naresh uncle for whom boundaries of acceptable behavior and words did not exist and whose ubiquitous cigars, hanging from smoke-darkened lips, filled the room with their pungent odor. At their parties, visiting architects from all over the world showed up, writers and artists came and went, discussions were animated, humor was ribald, cigarettes were smoked and always, always the whisky flowed. Rashna and I became enmeshed with these people, grew up with these friends of our parents and their children, followed their lives and successes, whispered about their excesses, and cried at their downfalls.

Often we were left at home with Mary while Mum and Paps went to yet another party, Mum gaily painting her eyelids an iridescent blue or green, and I urging her not to be such a show-off (for those were the years when I truly believed that my parents would have been much improved if they had just been invisible). After they left for one particular party at DM's and Uschi's, Mum excitedly anticipating seeing the English architect and his daughter, Deidre, who were making their annual visit (triumphantly: "lots of fun, baby, they are back"), Rashna and I felt a bit flattened, turning to homework dispiritedly and eating without complaint the haphazard dinner of badly-spiced, oily, fried pomfrets and watery French beans which Mary threw on the table like a challenge, asserting her full authority in the absence of the grown-ups.

Alone at home, Mary would sit in the darkened bedroom with us until we fell asleep, and sometimes she told us chilling stories about ghosts and banshees ("*Churails* will come to float around in your room and haunt you if you don't go to sleep just now, naughty girls!") that made us shiver inside and pretend that we were immediately asleep. In actuality, though, I would lie awake until I heard the key in the front door and Mummy and Paps's desultory swapping of the evening's events as they passed our room towards their own. The next day we hesitated to tell Mum about the *churail* story because Mary had pinched us hard in the past when we had tattled, but Rashna blurted it out. Mum scoffed loudly about the possibility of any such apparitions, shouted to Mary to keep her "stupid, *kamakli*, brainless stories" to herself (we were really in for a surreptitious pinching later, I thought ruefully, already rubbing my upper arms which would feel the brunt of her wrath), and asked us to use our brains which God had given us, what else were we being sent to such a good school, best in Bombay, for? Our relationship with Mary would be repaired, though, it always was. Mary cooked and cared for us and took our side if there was conflict between children and parents. In return, we shared neighborhood stories, taught her to read in English, and covered for her when she dressed up in her best clothes and vanished to meet her boyfriend when she should have been at home. When Mary went back to Mangalore, the South Indian city where so many of Bombay's domestic servants seemed to come from, to be married, we were desolate, unable to imagine our home without someone who had shared it for so many years, surprised but pleased that Mary had a life that was her own, and worried whether she would now be able to live it more fully, or face an uncertain future almost certain to be filled with hardship. We helped her select her trousseau and make her plans, almost as excited as she was, for our generation was becoming boldly free of the rigid class boundaries that had dictated life for previous Bombay generations.

Mum and Paps would go to multiple parties and dinners before they would agree that it was time that they had to host; it was just accepted that no one, least of all Mum and Paps, could compete with the prodigious party-giving capacity of the Camas. Then Paps would be in a tizzy, weighted down by the multi-partied obligations hanging around his neck like a noose, bringing out special crockery and cutlery, which had been banished to the far recesses of cupboards and sideboards, and Mum would plan a special menu. There had to be a mutton or chicken dish like *sali-murghi*, a mild chicken roasted with cumin, coriander, and caramelized onions with thin potato straws on top, a *tareli machhi*, a lightly-seasoned, pan-fried fish—pomfret, if in season—, vegetables, and a mutton *pulao* studded with cashews and redolent with a languorous and fragrant *dal* to go with it. Anything less would be shameful after so much hospitality received so many times over from the others. This was especially true of the Camas, who issued invitations to impromptu dinners at their place if no one else made a move, and did so repeatedly until someone did—their appetite for life and celebration seemingly endless. From them I have learned to try to embrace life in just such a manner—if there was no evident cause for celebration they created one, celebrating the Irani new year with fervor in addition to the Parsi one, both Parsi birthdays (calculated according to our ancient Zoroastrian calendars which were based on the birth of Zarathushtra, which scholars date between the 1100s B.C.E. and the 600s B.C.E.) and actual birthdays, and even borrowing celebrations from other communities, Christmas, Easter, Diwali in a continuous and repeating festive cycle.

Mum would supervise the kitchen for the first time in ages, her normal role being to abdicate all kitchen duties save the reciting of the daily menu to Mary (when she firmly told us that a woman's place was not in the kitchen, we had not stopped then to ask why Mary was consigned to it, the difficult and ever-present class issues only later being questioned and fulsomely opposed). And she would make her trifle, a deep-dished, multi-layered affair with cake, custard, fruit, and lashings of rum and fresh cream. This in particular we would hope against hope would be left over for the next day so that we could feast on it because, until our teenage years, we had to be in bed before the guests started arriving at nine-thirty. In true Bombay fashion, to arrive any earlier, even on a week day, was gauche and the parties lasted well past midnight. In my American life with its more limited social possibilities, and without the help of the ubiquitous cooks and maids, midnight-lasting dinners on week nights seem impossible. I wonder how our parents managed such elaborate nights so often and were still able to have the house up and running on time the next morning, a seamless tapestry of night and day, social and business, friends and family, and school and work that made up our Bombay life.

As the doorbell rang again and again Rashna and I shivered in delight and sometimes ran out into the drawing room only to dash back and report who had arrived. If we were caught, an aunty or uncle would surely "out" us and order us into the drawing room to be quizzed and questioned and otherwise prodded, so it was of supreme importance to swiftly run back into our beds again before we could be caught.

Once, the friends were invited during Diwali, the festival of lights and bursting firecrackers, which fact none of us were really concerned with except for the coincidental scheduling of the dinner party during this fortnight-long festival. As the usual guests started to arrive we knew something was wrong because we heard hushed voices rather than the usual ribald laughter. From the drawing room came muffled sobs, and then feet traipsing into Mum and Paps's bedroom followed by a series of anguished screams as other voices sought to soothe. As we girls dashed out, we learned that Uschi Aunty had received the full ear-splitting brunt of firecrackers and whistling rockets bursting wildly in our suburb in a way that never reached her ears on the high-high floor of her Walkeshwar flat that looked out onto Chowpatty, the shining Queen's Necklace, and the sea. The noise had evoked memories of bombs falling over her childhood hometown near Berlin, making her temporarily inconsolable. Only after all the windows had been shut and the noisy bedroom air-conditioner cranked up to its fullest in an attempt to drown out the fireworks, did she calm down and the party limp back to a semblance of normalcy.

Uschi Aunty's episode was discussed for years afterwards and Mum swore never to have another party in which DM and Uschi would be coming during Diwali. But Rashna and I looked at her with renewed interest, wondering again what she had left behind to begin her new life, no matter how gilded, with her new husband in what must surely have been an alien Bombay before she had made it her own. It was much, much later that we learned to relax in her presence, to not be apprehensive of the watery blue eyes that seemed to look through us, and the gruff German-accented English, and her many, many questions and commands. We began to enjoy her many-headed pursuit of books, music, and Indian culture and her dry, poker-faced Germanic humor, most of which was lost on the group, what with the accent and esoteric literary references. Uschi aunty definitely considered herself most discerning in literature and the arts, and I can now say that she indeed was, remembering as I do her eager dissection of the latest works by Indian authors—Salman Rushdie and Arundhati Roy and Vikram Seth—with anyone who was able and willing.

Even when I was already living in America and coming back only once a year, my ties with these friends and their children remained unbroken and we could pick up effortlessly where we had left off. Odder was the gradual morphing of our parents' friends into our own friends, the line between older and younger, parent and child, slowly blurring as the years wore on and as I eagerly turned to home to be revived with the seeming abandon of the whisky-cigar-laughter of their gatherings, to relive, if such a thing could be possible, my childhood past in the midst of a new and seemingly more restrictive American present. They, like my parents, were growing steadily older, although there was nothing amidst them to suggest or to give even a nod to it, nothing to bow or cave to or modify the lives they had led for all those decades past.

Some years after I left for America, DM had a massive heart attack after his customary evening drinks at Bombay Gymkhana (the friends raised glasses of Scotch at his memorial in the Il Palazzo flat) leaving Uschi to survive, first bewildered, and then accepting, in her borrowed-but-now-her land, another Baumgartner in Bombay. She was without her DM but with the constant support of this enduring, even if slowly dwindling, circle of friends and their children.

Many of Mum's and Paps's friends had weekend homes in nearby retreats to which our family had standing invitations: Poona, Panchgani, and of course the two favorites, Khandala and Lonavala, where many a Parsi sanatorium flourished for middle-class Parsis to take in the air, and the oldest Parsi bungalows were falling even then into slow disrepair. I imagined the old Khandala, already disappearing to newer buildings and more traffic, to have been as the slow-moving cities and towns of Anita Brookner's forgotten Europe with its displaced and startled protagonists—always too old, too foreign, too melancholy, too reminiscing, and too hesitant for the times, which had decidedly and rapidly moved on. One such bungalow, along the main Khandala-Lonavala Road just at the outside of Lonavala proper, we had watched every year become more and more dilapidated, shutters falling, windows pane-less and ajar, blackened paint chipping. It must have been magnificent in its time with a large front garden and many balconied rooms, but Mum said the family who inherited it embroiled it in a legal dispute over who the true heir was and the courts didn't render judgment for decades until the original players were dead and gone. We heard echoes of Homi Uncle's endless plaintiffs and defendants with their intricate and entrenched property sagas.

Later, these friends would also be the first to buy seafront and orchard property in Alibag and Awas, building homes of both traditional and modern design but always with large, open verandas, Parsi-style, on the new land. Alibag and Awas were once small villages of dirt roads, reachable across the sea from the ferries near the Gateway and the Taj Hotel and, of course, by car over the neglected highways. We grew up going to gentle old Khandala, so Rashna and I never took to Alibag's newness, rawness, and red dirt, or its lack of history and settled old community life, its dearth of Parsi bungalows and agiaries and genteel clubs. I understand now that property values have skyrocketed to undreamed-of heights and it is "the Hamptons of Mumbai" according to the Financial Times (which meets with hoots of incredulous laughter as I read the article aloud to Rashna).

I believe the pioneering spirit of Parsis in India, in Bombay, had propelled the generation of my parents, who were not tycoons, ship-builders, or businessmen as earlier generations of Parsis had been but rather architects, artists, doctors, and professionals, to seek out new land, build on it, and make it better than when they found it. The restlessness and courage that propelled the founding Paris from Iran centuries ago also propelled my parents' generation's forays into these newer areas. As to the displacement of villagers, class conflict, and rural poverty, those were conversations we children did not bring to the fore until much later, after we had gone to America, re-discovered India in ways we had not thought of before, and returned to live now-schizophrenic lives.

The Camas' home in Khandala was by no means among the oldest, but rather a Rusi Cama-designed, sprawling, mid-century modern with irregular roof-lines, uneven stone interior and exterior walls, open spaces, jutting terraces, and lawns that hugged and overlooked the steep ravine between their property and the main road bearing truck traffic and vacationers into Khandala. This Wright-inspired home I recognize in other suburban prototypes that I naturally gravitate to in my American city, their boldness and effortless blending of living and outdoor spaces filling me with memories of the Khandala home that Paps so honestly and openly admired and lauded his friend for. Once we rounded the curve of the very last *ghat* that tumbled you unceremoniously into Khandala, the Camas' bungalow appeared within a few minutes to the left over the deep ravine, a veritable Khandala landmark, and we hugged ourselves secretly because we knew we were there!

When we slept out on the broad, open veranda, the steady hum of constant traffic never left: a soothing, comforting, distant buzz that as much evoked Khandala for us as the roar of the ravine's running springs and quicksilver waterfalls, the coolness and mist of the monsoons, the insects—cacophonous crickets, clicking beetles—and the birds with their color and variety that we never saw in Bombay, confined as we were to sights of the depressed brown sparrow and tiresome black crow, the green parrots of earlier years having long disappeared.

These Khandala birds Mum followed with great pleasure, leaving the house early in the mornings for solitary walks or inviting us kids to join in, taking with her a dog-eared copy of noted ornithologist Salim Ali's guide to Maharashtra's birds. This practice of bird watching she carried on when visiting us in America years later, substituting Salim Ali's tome for one by the Audubon Society, taking my two boys in tow to discover birds in their back yard and neighborhood park that they had never really considered before. In life's inevitable irony, my boys followed her with wonder until they grew older, they too taking their own turn to withdraw from my mother and her enthusiasms in the way that I had so easily done decades ago. Not that I am concerned, so certain am I that they will return in their older years to the people and things that left their mark on them, just as I have.

I loved Khandala because it held its own rich and long history, a small village with a long past of some spectacular homes (now spectacular ruins as properties became too hard to maintain, fell into dispute, or families migrated out of India), and other modest but always tasteful ones. This was long before the tearing down of old, turn-of-the-century bungalows and the building of gaudy monstrosities, the strewing of debris and garbage by indiscriminate revelers, the impossible traffic jams on the main Khandala-Lonavala Road, and the discos and faux-Chinese restaurants built to accommodate the worst of Bombay tastes.

The *dasturji* family next door to the Camas, priests from Bombay, had a stone cottage lower and seemingly more precariously perched on the ravine and we kids would clamber over the stone fencing, knees grazing and rubber *chappals* flapping, to peer into the mothballed home with its antique, lacquered furniture piled atop one another and covered by linen bedsheets to protect from dust while the family was away. When they were in Khandala they would appear at the Camas' wide veranda for drinks and then would ensue Khandala-talk—about caretakers, upkeep of the house, water shortages, electricity cuts, and the corrupt local bureaucracy who constantly needed *baksheesh* to allow the smallest of improvements to the property. While Mum and Paps looked on with polite interest, I realized with relief and regret that these would never be our problems, as our cautious and circumspect father wouldn't buy a weekend home anywhere.

At the edge of the Camas' property, almost inside the ravine, a small stone pool was sometimes filled with water from a hose by the *mali*, and we dabbled our legs in it in delight, the exoticism of one's own swimming pool on one's own property being unknown in Bombay. The gardener would then proceed to caution us about the leopards and jackals that he had seen and heard in the ravine. We would chatter with excitement, and I would promise myself never to venture to this end of the property except with someone and in broad daylight, the very thought of roaming leopards making my heart thump with fear. Once Arman, the Camas' son, disappeared for many hours and I could tell that the family was growing edgy with concern even though they did not sound any alarms. I became convinced that he had been dragged away by a jackal, praying furiously that he would be returned without too much damage to limb. Eventually he was found on top of the long, sloping, disjointed roof. Needless to say, we all pounced with rage when the *mali* discovered him engrossed in a solo and silent game of all-out war on the rooftop, unconcerned at our fear.

Often other families and Uschi and DM, who had designed the first (and for decades, only) five-star hotel in Lonavala for his hotelier brother, would join the group, and we would make a convoy leaving Bombay, overnight bags, boxes, and cartons of food for two days stashed into three or four smallish cars with kids and adults squashed in between. In Panvel, the first and last stop before embarking on the then-harrowing bends of the *ghats* (now a new highway allows one to by-pass the *ghats* entirely and shorten the trip time, but also the excitement, by more than half), we would order *batata wadas,* hot round-round potato fritters with crispy tails and steaming chai, and the men would play their usual game of who would seize the check first in the age-old Indian ritual of not-allowing-friends-to-pick-up-the-tab-without-a-fight. Rusi Cama in his boisterous way would create a story around Paps's deft fingers, marveling at their uncanny swiftness to us children, and we would swell with pride for a while at Paps's prowess and magic fingers. For Paps it became almost a burden, so intent was he on swiping all the bills and paying for them, a small reciprocation for the endless generosity of the Camas, who not only took us, but also provided enormous amounts and varieties of food and drink that would be cooked and delicacies that would be served without limit: *mava* cakes, macaroons, *khari* biscuits to dip in tea, *choora*s made of puffed rice, spiced crisps, sultanas, and nuts; large salted cashews and almonds to go with the evening whiskies, cheese straws, and hand-made chocolates by Dadar Parsi Colony chocolatiers. No matter what Mum took with us—soft chicken patties from MacRonnels, chocolate cake made to order by her own Santacruz cake-maker-friend Juliet Vapose—it always paled in comparison to the sheer, endless variety of eatables appearing on the Cama end. Poor Paps, with so much pressure created by such munificence, he hardly ever tasted his *wadas* or tea in his eager watch for the check to appear.

Much of the weekend was spent on the veranda overlooking the ravine and the in-coming traffic. We kids lolled around at the outskirts of the adult group, sometimes joining in, sometimes willing them to forget about us, pulling out board games, reading our books through sultry afternoons where the breeze seemed to have stopped, exploring the lush and grassy terraces, or going for walks in the Khandala neighborhoods or to the decrepit Parsi sanatorium or to Rajmachi point, the highest in Khandala, where one could see clear across the whole of Khandala and wicked monkeys swayed and raced. Or going to DM's hotel to marvel and hang around like imposters while he completed some project or other, or going for ice creams to the close-by *bania* shop where I would quickly try to pay for them all in true Paps-fashion and in an effort to assuage my own chagrin at their largesse.

Sometimes as cars appeared on the main road across the ravine fresh from climbing the *ghats*, they would be friends and acquaintances of the Camas, other *Khandala-walas* with bungalows here and there, and they would hoot, scream, and wave from across the ravine as they rolled in, and we would all wave back, and I would secretly hope that they would not stop at the house, as they often did, because then the perfect magic moments with this group would be disturbed, the mood of tranquility destroyed, for they would have to be accommodated, fed, and their children played with and I would again be on the outside looking in, but this time perhaps not by choice.

In the evenings, we would pile into the cars again and go into Lonavala, to the bustling bazaar to buy bread, eggs, milk, choco-fudge, and pink *kopra pak* two famously sweet delicacies, the latter produced by Cooper's Chikki and made from burnt milk and coconut and sugar. This Parsi *chikki*-maker had been in Lonavala longer than any other (*chikk*i being a Lonavala delicacy), and although much reduced from the family's heyday, still did a brisk business. My favorite was cashew *chikki*, cashews encased in a hard honey-sugar shell that Mum always warned me against for fear of breaking my always-brittle teeth.

A few years later, Cooper's had been further reduced by a fire that had destroyed most of the shop, and I had not been able to shake the image of the flaming *chikki* shop with its burning packets of choco-fudge and *kopra pak* from my mind. "But how will they make up the money? How will they live? Are they poor? How did it catch fire? How much did they lose?" "*Arre Bbaba*, business people make up losses like that. They will be fine, see, the new shop is already open," Mum exasperatedly tried to reassure me. But the new shop was so much smaller, and now newer and swankier *chikki* makers—Maganlal's, National, and Friends—had become the foremost names in Lonavala *chikki* that people flocked to. I was convinced that an unshakable sadness engulfed the Cooper family behind the till, and I couldn't bear to see their faces or the shop again, preferring instead to hang out in the bowels of the bazaar, pretending to look at large, striped, canvas trader bags or hand-sewn leather *chappals* while the others bought packets and packets of *chikki* and fudge.

Sometimes we stopped at the Agiary in the middle of Lonavala market with its oasis-like garden of scented flowers and shrubs. Rusi Cama had done work over the years for the Agiary—tasteful additions, reconstructions and remodels, and he stopped to chat with the *dasturs* and trustees as we all tagged along, the tranquility enveloping us like a mist in the middle of the busiest tract of the town. Then, back home, cocktails with the indefatigable Zee Aunty's much-awaited goodies and soft drinks of choice for us kids, mango, raspberry, or ginger sodas made by Duke's (Parsi!), that we couldn't often get in Bombay. To keep the considerable mosquito onslaught at bay for the night, the *mali* and his two boys would set about making a fire of leaves and special herbs that were meant to ward off the mosquitoes and which evidently worked, because I don't recall being bitten any of those times. Mattresses were laid side by side in the great drawing room and we would sleep many to the room, its long, shuttered windows and doors eventually closed against any animal that might wander in, as a buffalo once did, causing much consternation, hilarity, and fleeing of sleep before it was collectively shooed out, ambling out of the main gates, and back towards the village again.

Chapter 10

Excellent Women

During World War II, as England survived aerial bombardment, rationing, misery, and want, they were sustained in part by their Land Girls and "excellent women." While the men (and some women) fought and died on European soil, these women held the fort in villages, towns, and cities across England, becoming, as enshrined in the books of E. M. Forster, Barbara Pym, or Dora Saint, the unseen glue that held together English life and, in the case of the Land Girls, ensured that the country's soil would yield food to eat. In the aftermath of the war, they eschewed a future that might hold husbands, children, and families and built, if unknowingly, a future for their country instead, a base from which to go forward out of the rubble and loss. Giving unsentimental strength to wives and mothers who had lost husbands and children, filling the churches' pews with their steadfast faith and the churches' vases with flowers from their gardens, and organizing fetes and fairs for the children, these excellent women quietly gave courage while creating the stability for English life to carry on. All over the world, excellent women made their invaluable contributions without which the lives of everyone would have been so much poorer. Where challenge, hardship, or oppression existed—as in America during slavery and the civil rights eras—strong women, the women who filled Alice Walker's, Gloria Naylor's, and Toni Morrison's novels, arose, holding together children and families, keeping traditions, and mending spirits so that life could go on amidst injustice.

In Bombay, we too had our own excellent women in ample measure and in every community. Indian women like Sarojini Naidu, Rani Laxmibai, and Bhikaiji Cama had given courage while India fought for the British during World Wars I and II. They fought both from the sidelines and at the helm of the Indian independence struggle, which attained its goal of a free India two years after the war ended. Steeped in the strength of their own Indian-Victorian upbringing and single from the demographic realities of Parsi life, our own life was studded by these women. Most excellent of all was my Great-Aunt Roda, surrogate grandmother when Mamina had died young and suddenly, a steady presence, quiet listener, courageous rationalist, and surprisingly young heart.

Roda had grown up in the sprawling homestead of Palamkot Hall. The home held impossibly vast rooms, gangplank-like balconies, dusty, ebonized furniture of old-time visage like the swan-handled *chaise longue* and miniature Victorian chairs meant for small derrieres that we kids fitted ourselves into, and massive, lion-pawed dining table. Piled in an unadorned show-case were Wedgwood and Japanware services and tarnishing silver cutlery in their walnut chests. Four mosaic-tiled open terraces jutted from the bedrooms and kitchen, overlooking Dadar Parsi Colony's red-tiled roofs and tiered balconies, and the green, pristine Five Gardens. Around these five separate verdurous gardens, the colony was built. Dadar Parsi Colony was a small village that was of a rapidly-fading Bombay. Low buildings housed huge flats with balconies adorned with Greco-Roman colonnades, cherubs, gargoyles, and *farohars*, the ancient Persian guardian angels. Sloping tiled red roofs with missing tiles recalled Italianate villages. The colony also held gardens, squares, a vast Agiary with green bushes and flowering plants set in the midst of well-laid-out streets, schools, lending libraries where my Roda was a regular, an orphanage where little Parsi boys with small velvet *topis* on their heads studied to become *dasturs*, and of course the Dadar Parsi Gymkhana where almost every evening of Roda Aunty's life, she sat in a wicker chair looking over the expanse of shabby brown lawn with her circle of friends, couples, families, and other excellent women like herself.

The colony was almost entirely Parsi, where pious *mathabanoo*-clad women scurried in their long, cotton skirt-blouses to offer prayers at their Agiary and hip young girls paraded the Five Gardens in shorts and miniskirts while boys revved up motorcycles in chase around the encircling lanes, much as it was during Gool's time there. Even today, the colony retains this quality of an astonishing other world in the middle of Mumbai. But it is tired now, many of the buildings in disrepair, many of the walkers old and unmoored, and a general sense of melancholia of a dying community and closing era hovers in the air. Orhan Pamuk's "hüzün" wafts like a ghost through the old magnificence. Pamuk's evoking of the sense of loss scenting Istanbul with its centuries of history and the Ottoman Empire's vanished glory mirrors the painful reminiscence of a disappearing past in the Dadar Parsi Colony. It is palpable now, although it is nameless: our own "hüzün," our air of retreat, our "Parsiana."

While taking care of her parents at Palamkot Hall, Roda also took care of my mother when she was a child and when Mamina became pre-occupied with Mina. Mum grew up in those big rooms and leafy Dadar lanes, gathering friends, living with grandparents and cousins, holding dear this aunt who kept her unsentimental and tolerant eye always on her, and made Mum the center of her existence in a way that perhaps her mother couldn't at the time. Eventually, Mummy went back to Khalakdina Terrace and began college at St. Xavier's. Roda's parents died and her siblings got married and moved away save one, Rusi. Rusi Uncle lived in eccentric isolation in Palamkot in the interim years while Roda taught for decades at Mahalaxmi's sea-facing Happy Home and School for the Blind (the only such residential school of its kind in Bombay that I knew of) under Principal Meher Banaji's (undoubtedly another excellent woman) able reign.

At Happy Home, Rashna and I visited our aunt as children, bunking overnight in her small en suite room, which faced the busy road lined by Mahalaxmi Race Course and the Haji Ali Mosque further down in the Arabian sea. In the evenings, we strolled down the sea-face to watch the restless grey waves and to eat at the corner Chinese restaurant. In her room, Roda had a single bed, a desk and chairs, a cupboard, and a small stove on which to heat tea, coffee, and soups. I'm not even sure how we fit, all three of us, in that small room but we found it thrilling, deeply comforting, to be with Roda with her calm presence and no-nonsense responses to our fanciful outbursts. We cautiously eyed the milky-eyed girls who roamed the school's corridors, laughing and tittering and swaying in their blindness and calling out, "Roda tai, Roda tai"—their very own Roda Aunty. It was terrifying to bump into the girls and answer their questions when they sensed our presence and called out, catching us edging past them and sensing our shame at our fear. Roda unsentimentally instructed us that there was nothing to be afraid of or sad for, that these girls had adjusted to their blindness and were grateful to be receiving good educations and planning careers, and that we must treat them like any other girls their age and be grateful for our own good fortunes.

Being from Mum's side of the family, Roda had never learnt to cook. As Mum was fond of repeating, "Women were not meant to be in the kitchen." The cook at the family's Palamkot Hall home, Pema, who lived with his family in quarters downstairs across the courtyard, made for many years, at our specific lunch request, the same *gravy na cutlace* which evoked the rich and juicy meat cutlets of Mamina's Khalakdina Terrace kitchen, all smothered in the unforgettable, spicy-sweet tomato gravy. Roda outlived the old Palamkot Hall retainers, and her own ascetic independence didn't quite allow for them anyway. So after Pema was long gone, my aunt survived on packed *bhonu*, a Parsi version of the fresh-made meals that cooks put into *dabbas* and *tiffins* and *dabbawallas* deliver to offices and schools all over Bombay. Hers arrived from the kitchen of an enterprising neighbor and was hand-delivered each day. Thus she stayed true to the last to the Rustom maxim that a woman's place was anywhere but the kitchen!

After she retired from Happy Home, Roda returned to the only other home she had ever known, Palamkot Hall. Here the necessary adjustments were made with Rusi Uncle who had gone from eccentric to worse—sometimes showing up completely naked and shaking with laughter as Roda hastily averted her eyes as he methodically turned on every light in the house and cranked up the radio in a maddening routine. But brother and sister co-existed, although Roda did grumble at Rusi's repeated creation of annoyance and chaos.

Some small improvements were made to make the flat livable for Roda again. The old furniture had to be dusted, the kitchen made to function again, but other than that, Roda Aunty left well alone, was content to be back in her spacious bedroom with its own terrace and an enormous balcony, where high cane-backed chairs overlooked the Five Gardens. Roda enjoyed the momentary noise and laughter when we went for lunch, as we would delightedly spot one or two of the Camas walking their dog around the garden's periphery or as Mum would see some of her numerous old school friends and call out noisily while we shrank with embarrassment.

Unable and unwilling to live a simple life of retirement, Roda worked at the National Association for the Blind (NAB) in town for the next thirty years of her life, going to all of Bombay's schools in turn, and working with their Interact Clubs, Scouts, and Girl Guides to raise money for the NAB. Incredibly, her trip to work from Palamkot involved a good fifteen minute walk on pitted roads to Wadala station and a train to Victoria Terminus every day, an hour-long journey which leaves even the young and energetic sapped of strength and wilting, but I never saw Roda tired. At work she unceremoniously made unlikely new friends with her co-workers, friends from distant suburbs who traveled two hours by train because they needed this job and who were far removed from her early life in Palamkot's splendor. These friends, in addition to her daily companions at the Dadar Parsi Gymkhana and other relatives in far-flung corners, whom we had ceased to visit but she still did, all had a place in Roda's orderly life. Sometimes we would hear her sharing with Mum snippets of their lives—abusive husbands, crushing debts, failing children—that she had been asked to advise on and help with, and which she unfailingly did.

In the evenings after returning home from work, she would walk the twenty minutes to the Parsi Gymkhana, finally returning home for the night well after nine. Such a pace would have killed us. On Saturdays, she would make this entire trip to work, leave before lunch (it was Saturday half-day), take the train back to Bandra station and then board a bus to see us. As she turned seventy and then eighty, we were increasingly doubtful and incredulous. "Roda Aunty, when will you retire? Now come on, don't you want to relax more? Aren't you tired?" She would respond that she didn't need to relax more and that if she didn't do her work, what else would she do. Her famous stoic response: "…and so, what of it?" dismissed all doubtful questions about her perceived (only by us) hardships and ailments and aches. Without knowing of them, Roda Aunty had adopted the Stoic philosophy: to change what you can and to accept serenely what you can't, without excuses, laments, regrets—and always, always, to live with dignity, to live well, because you were your own final judge. Roda would have made the Stoic emperor Marcus Aurelius proud, proving in her own way the truth of his musing that "even in a palace, it is possible to live a good life." For Roda Aunty, it was an impossibility to not live a good life anywhere.

Until her ninetieth birthday, Roda continued this schedule, which for the rest of us was unthinkable, mad, to say the least, but for her was just a normal workday. To celebrate her milestone birthday, we had a dinner party for her at Palamkot where relatives were invited and the terraces were thrown open to hold the guests. The tall cane-backed chairs were pushed to one end of the veranda by my relentlessly energetic first-born, so that both my American-Indian-Parsi boys, who were visiting during their summer holidays, could play cricket with her on the broad and dusty veranda facing Five Gardens. He shouted, "One more ball, one more, come on!" to Roda Aunty, which she would obediently throw, and he would swipe wildly at it, baseball-style, with his cricket bat. Assorted uncles and aunties squealed with mirth and some concern for Roda as she threw ball after ball with bony arms before proclaiming herself "a little tired" and in need of a short rest. Roda Aunty's nephew from London, whom she was greatly fond of, called in to wish her happy birthday at that point, and we sang "for she's a jolly good fellow," and the rest of the cricket game was thankfully forgotten.

A few months after this, Roda, who had never had a sickness or been to a hospital in her life, suffered a series of strokes. She battled back, struggling to retain control over her walk, speech, and movements as Mum spent more and more time with her. From America, we made anxious phone calls and exhorted her to keep fighting (as if we needed to). In my last call to her, Mum handed her the phone and I imagined them both sitting on the tall, cane-backed chairs facing the Gardens as we talked. Biting back my fears, I told her I would see her soon and signed off saying, "Keep your spirits up, Roda Aunty!" and she replied, predictably, "Oh, yes!" as if there could be no other response. I was convinced that she would be well again, taking the train and bus to see Mummy on all upcoming Saturdays as usual, forever, or at least until I could make my next trip back and see her again, spindly legs sticking out of one of the five or six always-sleeveless faded cotton dresses she wore ("Too hot for sleeves in Bombay," she would aver), soft wispy white hair flying a little in the breeze, sensible flat sandals, cotton *thela* that held umbrella, book—no newspaper, for she lived frugally and saved in the least likely of places ("You see, I can always read the paper at work, at your house, or at the Gymkhana")—and other items that might be needed for the day.

In the week before she had her massive heart attack, Mum got a call from the day-and-night aide who had been employed for Roda Aunty, saying that Roda had insisted on walking to the Gymkhana in the evening, had become disoriented, had sat down on the sidewalk as passersby gathered, and that they had got her back to her feet with much difficulty and taken her home. I am now sure that this was the only thing that Roda had ever feared in her life: that she would someday not be able to take care of herself, that she would be a burden on Mum, that she would have to surrender the independence of nine decades and be beholden to someone else, even if it was the little girl she had raised and who loved her with an unreserved and grateful heart. I'm glad that she never had to actually live with that fear come true. For the strokes, dependency, and heart attack all moved swiftly through her life, taking up only the last three months of her ninety years—most of which she was quite unaware of.

Afterwards, as Mummy made the rounds to her bank and utilities companies and tied up loose ends, she was astonished to learn that Roda, who had always fiercely rejected our offer to give her money for taxis, trips, microwaves, or any of the big and small things that might have made for a more comfortable existence to ordinary folks, and who had in her own lifetime given away to her own nieces, nephews, and their children everything of value she had ever owned (all her jewelry, diamonds and emeralds and rubies), had a mere lakh of rupees in her savings account. Such a laughable sum might have made others in her position seek help or sicken with anxiety or worry about the future, but Roda had never let it upset her because she was convinced that she would never need to draw on that small sum, that she would work until the end. She would look after herself; she would never give up control of the life she had fought to create for herself from a cosseted and gilded childhood into the reality of the new, post-independence India.

In all the years that Roda faithfully came to our Santacruz abode on Saturdays, all the times we spent overnight or for lunch at Palamkot Hall, all the trips she took us on across India with her Dadar group of excellent fellow travelers, through all our years in America where she ended each rough blue aerogramme letter with "longing to see you again," and on our annual trips back home, as we grew from girls into women, as her hair turned from grey-streaked black to salt-and-pepper and then snowy white, through it all, our Roda Aunty was a constant in our lives, growing more precious with each advancing year. Once she asked me to trim her hair, as her regular hair cutter was on vacation and she didn't know where else to go. I remember taking the insubstantial silky strands in my hands and being flooded with an unbearable pity and love as the soft locks wound themselves around my heart. I willed myself to give her the best haircut she had ever had, although in the end she looked as she always did.

We never heard my aunt say anything bitter, vile, or envious, never engage in cruel gossip. We never heard her lament any possible loneliness stemming from her single status in a country where marriage was considered the norm and single women curiosities; indeed she was fiercely independent, valuing greatly her self-sufficiency and perhaps even her singleness. She never made us feel guilty when we fled the house on *her* Saturdays because we had more important and exciting dates for the evening ahead. We never saw her depressed, melancholy, sentimental, or anything other than serene, cheerful, fully equipped to face the world, and—travel being the only luxury she afforded herself—face it she did. Of all the assorted uncles and aunties who cram and enrich an Indian life and who certainly crowded ours, Roda Aunty was the only one in the world, other than Mum and Paps, to whom we were first, were everything, and we were secretly and shamefully glad that she had no one else, that we had her all to ourselves, no competition, just us.

When I returned to Bombay a few months later, Mum handed me a pair of big round Burmese ruby earrings, the only jewelry that we had ever known Roda to wear daily, her ringless fingers and bony bare wrists deliberately free of the entanglement of bracelets and bangles in a country where these become extra appendages for most women, heavy golden oppression. The earrings she had wanted me to have. I've only worn them once but gaze on them often. Somehow, they don't suit me quite the same as they did my Roda, on whose thin, protuberant ears (that Paps had affectionately scoffed were another unfortunate trademark of Mum's family), they sat with confidence and at complete ease with the old cotton dresses and frayed sandals and hanging threadbare cloth bag. In them, I feel like an imposter, quite unequal to my excellent aunt.

When I am back in our West Breeze flat and the doorbell rings, I sometimes rush to open the door, momentarily convinced that on the other side will be Roda coming for her faithful Saturday visit, frail and bony, all thin and dangling arms and legs, fanning herself with her hanky and waiting impatiently for her Tinaz to let her in.

Chapter 11

BOMBAY BIRTHDAYS

Birthday celebrations started early at West Breeze-Sea Breeze. Before we children were quite awake, the doorbell would ring repeatedly, signaling that our birthday was here! The *mali* would deliver small presents from our aunties and uncles from *passay* and upstairs. These were often eclectic and unpredictable, and not your standard children's presents, toys, or games; when we rushed to tear open the packages, they revealed bits of embroidery, or crochet hankies and collars, or papier-mâché lanterns, or intricately hand-carved candles in blushing colors that my aunties worked on, or a tiny beaded purse—small, beautiful items that somehow invoked our shared Pavri past and that I accepted with pleasure.

Even school was faced with anticipation as I deliciously hugged to myself the knowledge that we would be celebrating, as my family always did, with a Chinese dinner later. And of course it was a day when the teachers seemed kinder in acknowledgment of one's special day, and everyone wanted to be your best friend as you importantly handed out sweeties and toffees from large plastic bags to your classmates at the designated time. Other students may go overboard, doling out pencils and erasers, and the Bollywood kids in school would even give whole pencil boxes filled with everything we could ever want—rulers, felt-pens, and protractors (oh, how we hoped for the film kids to be in our classes!)—but we knew that our parents would have condemned such drawings of attention to oneself, birthday or not.

On our birthdays, we would be given special privileges, like first dibs on the afternoon papers. Paps would bring home the afternoon dailies when he came home at seven, and if we were home, buried in our homework or just whiling away time reading or lounging, Rashna and I would rush to open the door for him to snatch away the rags, delicious to read with evening coffee. Usually the nimblest that day won, with Paps bemused as always by our ardor for newspaper, but on a birthday, the birthday girl always won. Then, I would slowly read my favorite pieces and end, always, with "Busybee's" column, which first appeared in *Mid-Day*, and then, after he bought and launched his own paper, *The Afternoon Despatch & Courier*. In our house, his finest columns became a piece of evening conversation. "Did you read 'Busybee' today? *Vanchyu-ke?*" Or, if it was a particularly uninspired one, "Chee, what has he written today, all rubbish. Sometimes he just writes anything!" And Behram Contractor, a thickly-lensed, awkward, stooped, middle-aged journalist of modest prior repute improbably became keeper of Bombay history, chronicler of her foibles, loving if ironic holder of her stories, an unlikely hero, along with the cartoonists R.K. Laxman and Mario Miranda, who doodled and scrawled and created with unerring skill our Bombay life in stick figures and color. Everyone had their favorite "Busybee" column, and I had so many: his musings on the vanishing Irani restaurants with their Parisian-café-like wooden tables, chairs, glass-fronted cupboards, and mixed-Parsi-Irani fare; on the local trains with their daily soap-operas conducted within; on venerable institutions like the Asiatic Society and the beautiful goddess Flora who gave busy Flora Fountain its name; and on old Parsis stooped around the sacred Bhikha Behram Well in Fort while tying their *sudra-kusti* and mumbling their ancient prayers in Avesta, a language few had heard of; vignettes of Bombay life that its citizens understood instinctively and well and held fast to.

Also on our birthday evenings, Mary would put out a new birthday dress, usually purchased by Paps for his girls with his discerning artist's eye. We never minded changing on birthdays, even though changing every day for the evening was a different matter, as we, like many Indian boys and girls, were forced to change into "evening clothes" by our mothers, even if it was just for a stroll in the lanes close by or a walk to the nearby Rotary park, where other little children would gather and shriek, and the maids would chat and commiserate and eat *channa-sing* from newspaper cones until the dusk fell, regularly at seven. In my American life, I always find the change of time over different months disconcerting. Spring forward…fall backward…sometimes dark at five, sometimes dark at nine; it's so difficult to bring to this life permanence and the surety of a Bombay life where the sun invariably rose and set around seven. Now, after I return to the U.S., my internal clock is dislocated for weeks, seeking dimness and the close of day when there is a gay and bright light outside, beckoning, forcing, mocking if you have already retreated.

Getting dressed for the evening also meant shoes and socks, no sandals or *chappals* allowed. Often, other friends were allowed to skip the shoes and socks, but never us, not until later when we became teenagers and rebelled, and there was a showdown, and I (as I often did) won. Then, I could wear slip-ons and open toes and even rubber *chappals*, because

Mum and Paps had conceded this battle for more important ones. And, by then, these neo-Victorian practices were beginning to recede in Indian households and even in Parsi ones.

And before we could go out for the evening, birthday or not, we had to have our drink at teatime. While the mummies and aunties would have their cups of tea with small plates of *ganthia* and cream or chocolate biscuits, or leafy, spicy fried *patrel* and small, rich *mava* cakes—sweet and savory, *tikhu-mithu* perfectly balanced—we children had to drink our "milk," which could be Bournvita or Horlicks only, hot-hot with a disagreeable froth on the top that made us gag when it wasn't sweetened enough to be palatable. But drink it we must, because otherwise our bones wouldn't grow and our skin wouldn't shine and we would remain *nulhu-nulhu*, "small-small," forever. We got our milk from the *dudhwala* who came to the house with the stainless steel pails of fresh milk—whole, skim, and cream. We would hold out our *tapelas* as he would slowly and ever so carefully measure out the amount we wanted with his long-handled ladle, letting each scoop fall in grand cascades into the proffered pan. That unpasteurized milk would then immediately be boiled, cooled, and then stored in the fridge for use until the next day.

Birthday teas were further supplemented by the *bakerywallah's* offerings. He labored up our long broad flight of stairs with his rusty, peeling red crate perfectly balanced on his head. God knows how long he had already walked and how far he still had to go! Mum always clucked with sympathy and immediately brought him a cold drink when he appeared at the door, panting a little from his efforts and mopping his brow with the coiled cloth that cushioned his head from the heavy steel crate. And when he unpacked his multi-layered crate and displayed his goods, we always bought from him whether we wanted some or not, because he knew all our birthdays and always appeared on them, without fail, to make his sales and collect his baksheesh. Mutton *pattice*, chocolate rum *babas* (without any rum, of course, where would a poor *bakerywallah* like him get *babas* with real rum?), rectangular cream cakes in white and pink and lurid yellow, and sometimes chicken and mutton rolls, oily and spicy and nothing in comparison to Hearsch Bakery's at Hill Road or Paradise Café's in Colaba (the ultimate in gooey, fresh-pale yellow-mayonnaise-enfolded chicken rolls). But these lesser ones would get eaten over teatime or Mum and Paps's evening coffee, and then later left for Mary or Savitribai, our daily maid and their friends, to finish. Sometimes, they would be bought simply to be given away, because of course *bakerywallah* couldn't be expected to come up all those steps and not make a substantial sale. Globalization has now created chic cafés for those of means and lesser ones for those of more modest budgets, effectively edging out these *bakerywallahs* from Mumbai lives.

Also vanished from the new Mumbai are the men who came once a year with a crate full of laces, buttons, frills, and ribbons, and one of whom we called the *Kabuliwallah* because he spoke of making his annual journey from Afghanistan through the northwest towards Bombay. We found it thrilling and adventurous and almost unbelievable because we had never met anyone who had been to Afghanistan before, or Pakistan, or anywhere in northern India for that matter, although like most people we knew, we had many, many scattered relatives and friends across Europe and America, part of the Parsi and Indian diasporas. Mum, who was a surprisingly excellent seamstress, bought many of the fragile lace pieces, colorful ribbons, and buttons for her sewing, which included the cutting and stitching of new dresses for herself, Roda Aunty, or us (until we firmly declined to wear her hand-sewn couture outside). Rashna and I skirmished over which two pieces we could choose for ourselves and as usual, I ended up threatening her with dire alternatives until she agreed to my choice. Then, Mum peppered the *Kabuliwallah* with questions about his journeys and he would sigh and shake his head and say, "*Arre,* what can I tell you, *memsaab*, it is getting harder and harder to make a life like this. In Afghanistan, now there is lots of fighting!" *Kabuliwallah* always got a hot cup of tea and the exhortation to "stay, stay and take some rest before you go out again!" And one year, he simply stopped coming. Afghanistan was starting its descent into hell.

Birthdays meant Chinese dinner with the family. And for us it meant MacRonnel's, which served as our resident Bandra bakery-café-Chinese restaurant before there were delis and coffee houses and organic bakeries and the many, many types of specialty-Chinese restaurants that now showcase so much beyond the generic fare that we thrilled at before the new globalization. Standing opposite St. Stanislaus on Hill Road, MacRonnel's was run by a Christian family, embedded in the history of Bandra's lanes and by-lanes. The handsome and immaculately maintained stone-carved St. Stanislaus had been Paps's school, and this he proudly and redundantly pointed out each time we went to MacRonnel's, to which we rolled our eyes and sniffed, "Bombay Scottish is the best." In the new Mumbai, in a surprising development, many of the old Catholic schools have now taken over the education of young impoverished Muslims, while other communities have fled to other schools in an underlining of the increasing polarization and alienation of the city's community life that was never apparent to us then.

For their chicken and mutton patties, their cakes and pastries, and the little chicken-salad-in-pastry boats, which were widely accepted as the best in Bandra, we went to MacRonnel's. But it was its Chinese and birthday avatar that I best remember MacRonnel's for. Eating out was not the reflexive activity it has become in my American life and, in the new Mumbai, thoughtlessly engaged in because time is short and life, to repeat that great inanity, is busy. We rarely ate out then—it was always for celebratory occasions—and we deliciously anticipated the event for days before. Our MacRonnel's menu selection stubbornly stayed the same over the years because we didn't wear it out with frequent use: sweet corn and crab soup to start (not the chicken version, which we agreed was lesser than the flaky, sweet shards of fresh, delicate crab); American chop suey with its gooey, lurid red-clad noodles crowned by a glistening fried egg, which we girls refused to touch but Mum gladly accepted, her love of eggs being trumped only by her love of cheese; fried rice (whether it would be mixed meats or just chicken would take many minutes to decide: if chicken, we would be guaranteed plentiful juicy bits of chicken, but if mixed, we would get the variety of chicken, pork, and prawns, but perhaps not quite in the same quantity…); and sweet and sour pork with chunks of pineapple and luscious, fried pork morsels. Drinks were ordered all around, and we would leave sated. One of the MacRonnel brothers always came over to our table to greet us on these celebratory dinners, and Mum anticipated this with pleasure. "These Christians are such nice people, friendly and honest," she would say approvingly, freely stereotyping the characteristics of different communities, as all Indians did. Accordingly, a community might be good at business, brainy, happy-go-lucky, eccentric, hot-headed, or brave and warrior-like; of course, not all stereotypes that Indians engaged in would be flattering, but poisonous stereotypes were never allowed nor uttered in my family. Indeed, Bandra was filled with the Christians—MacRonnels, DeSouzas, Braganzas, and Regos—their churches, schools, bakeries, and cold storage shops that sold deli and other meats. Beside MacRonnel's was the other Bandra Chinese restaurant, Gazebo, with its slightly gaudy exterior and businessman types who frequented it. This was never our choice while the sweet MacRonnel's remained in existence; we did not have a relationship with the owners of Gazebo, who were not present in the restaurant anyway, the way we had established with the MacRonnels. These restaurants, the Parsi Dairy *kulfi* cart across the road for sweet, cold, creamy burnt-milk ices to cap off the evening, and other assorted ice cream shops around where youngsters gathered, made Hill Road lively late into the night.

    Beggars waited patiently outside these establishments with their palms extended and their voices pleading. Every Bombayite of means lived in the uneasy juxtaposition of one's comfortable life and the deprivation one saw all around them—hungry children with distended stomachs and disheveled hair brown from dirt, women in rags hugging babies to withered breasts, lepers who expertly wheeled themselves around on small makeshift carts because they had lost their limbs to the disease, and other slum children who might have eaten that day and were therefore ready to sing a Hindi film song with a gusto that defied their precarious existence. These children were not beyond lustily mocking us—the other—those with money to eat with and live by, by slyly calling us actors and actresses we knew we looked nothing like. "Oi, look, Zeenat Aman! Hallo, aunty!" they would cry, "Look at that hero, *bilkul* Rajesh Khanna, hallo Mr. Rajesh Khanna!" to a large-stomached middle-aged man, quite the opposite of the dashing Bollywood star. Once when we stepped out from my birthday dinner, I saw people gathering and dispersing outside as usual, some with ice creams in their hands, neatly stepping over what appeared to be a supine beggar, ill, drunk, or dead. I tried to shut out the image, along with countless others of desperate Bombayites, but these become part of the Bombay photo book of one's memories which pop out uninvited on unexpected occasions.

Very rarely, if our birthday fell on a weekend, we might go to the Taj Mahal Hotel in Colaba, which, along with the Oberoi's at Nariman Point, seemed to be the only two five-star hotels in Bombay, or at least the only two that mattered. For Parsis, of course, there was only one five-star, and that was the Taj. Built by the Tatas in 1903, the Taj spanned two huge sea-fronting blocks just steps away from the Gateway of India. That once-imposing entry had literally been a ceremonial gateway into Bombay from the Arabian Sea. Its massive arches were built in 1911 for the visit of Queen Mary and King George the V, and by the 1980s, it was decayed, broken, and defaced by neglect and the unfettered stomping of millions of feet through its open passageways looking out to sea. Today, some of this entry traffic is restricted, but for the Gateway, as for much of Mumbai, it seems both too little and too late; too little and too late to make a dent in the unbridled and daunting mess that has now become the city. But near the Gateway, the Taj has survived and thrived, still-shining in all its serene glory despite the desperate 26/11 terrorist attempt to burn it to the ground, to reduce it to rubble, and try to erase it forever.

To the Taj we went, only for the most vaunted of celebrations, for it was even then prohibitively expensive with the socialist government's added luxury taxes distending bills to what were to us eye-popping totals. In addition to the rare birthday celebration, these events included the weddings and *navjotes* of wealthy relatives and friends, and special occasions, as when Paps's favorite sister Kashmira visited from abroad. I remember one birthday when we invited her and my cousins, and we all piled into our trusty Fiat for tea at the Taj. Nothing was too good for the charming Kashmira, Paps's youngest sibling, once a beauty queen of the Masina hospital ball ("Parsi-built, *baebee*") and Paps's companion through his days at the J.J. School of Art. Kashmira was the princess all his friends clamored for, those same friends who grew to become some of Bombay's most well known architects, and remained our family friends over the decades.

In the Sea Lounge of the Taj, with its long windows overlooking the choppy expanse of grey sea across and the dirt-encrusted Gateway that loomed to its left, Kashmira Aunty ordered beans on toast and *bhel-puri*, the latter street food having been proclaimed safe to eat within the Taj's sanitized walls (made with bottled water, *dikra*). Looking around in delight because we were the ones with the "foreign" relatives, I didn't even resent the strictly liquid diet Mum had restricted us to ordering before we left home. Friana and Fareshte, our cousins of whose clothes and accents we were equally in awe, would pick at their sandwiches as Rashna and I would order Thums Up and Limca under Mum's watchful eye. In the Sea Lounge, old Parsi men and women drank tea, ate three-scooped Risky Rider ice cream in their silver boats, and chatted with the waiters, some of whom had been with the hotel for decades and others who had just started what would be lifetime careers. Among these must surely have been some of the brave Taj work-staff who died in the harrowing events of 26/11, unthinkably giving up their own lives to protect the lives of hotel guests. In the background, fittingly for this mellow and older crowd, the pianist played "Last Waltz" and "Begin the Beguine," and Mum waxed approving. My friends laughed at the thought of going to the Sea Lounge because it was so un-hip, and would only deign to go to the Taj for its disco (for in the eighties discos were only attached to hotels and not anywhere and everywhere as clubs, bars, and pubs now are). But I loved that vast, columned, sedate room with its muffled chatter, tinkling piano, familiar waiters, soft courtesy, and opulent ice cream boats.

In the new Mumbai, there are so many new five-star hotels that I haven't kept count. Many are fabulous, giving competition to the best hotels anywhere, but their sleek, cosmopolitan glass-chrome-waterfall interiors could be anywhere. At the Taj, you can never mistake where you are, for time stops a little and you are forced to slow down and look at the magnificent wood-and-wrought-iron staircase leading to the Sea Lounge, or the lovingly polished antique wood table emitting a soft glow, or gaze outside at the old Gateway and the sea beyond. And even though five-star, access to it, even if only to sit in the lobby, seems more open to all classes than in other hotels, and even though hit by terrorist attacks, it is as embracing as before. As for the warm, impeccable, and incomparable service, one can find it still, not just at my Taj in Colaba, but also at any Taj Hotel anywhere in India.

Best of all was when one's birthday coincided with an unexpected holiday, a Bombay *bandh*, when the city would be ordered/forced closed (*bandh* literally meaning closed) by various political actors or parties over irreconcilable grievances, or a bank holiday, or a monsoon rain-holiday. Then, the birthday would stretch deliciously and one would not have to hurry to school. On a monsoon rain holiday, the skies would crash, bang, and pour out sheets and sheets of loud, clamorous rain all through the night. If you woke up (as you almost inevitably did) to a particularly violent clap of thunder and heard the relentless pouring outside your windows (for windows could be left wide open through the night because there was no malaria and dengue in Bombay then as is, ironically, rampant in the sophisticated new Mumbai now), you would smile sleepily and bury your face further into a pillow made unusually cool by the driving water outside, hoping against hope that the floods were high enough for school to be declared closed the next morning. And then you got word (How? Void of Internet, TV, cell phones, and hardly even any landlines, this seems almost inconceivable and mysteriously magical now) that school *was* closed! It was closed and trains were closed; the whole city seemed to be closed. Oh, the pleasure of going back into your cool, cool bed and, for that moment, not thinking of math or biology tests and simply savoring time itself. Then, the birthday would begin. Breakfast would be ordered from Mary—not the usual dry-burnt toast and milky tea with porridge and half-boiled eggs, but real eggs, perhaps a *pora*, an omelette made thick with onions, cilantro, chilies, and redolent of cumin and turmeric. For you completely lost your usual anxiety-induced nausea for the coming school day and could easily eat one, two, three eggs, or the celebratory *pora*.

You looked out of the veranda windows with delight onto a brown, rippling ocean that filled the compound, the lanes, roads, and everything beyond. With the neighborhood gang, who called out your name and sang happy birthday outside the front of the building, you ventured outside with pants folded up high and walked the streets getting steadily soaked even though Paps had warned you against going ("See, you will fall down and be dragged away somewhere, be careful!"). And really, this wasn't just Paps's usual pessimism and restriction, because both Kobad Uncle and then Mum herself had on previous occasion fallen into an open manhole when the water was high and been saved only when alert passersby had spied their outthrust limbs and, in Mum's case, an open umbrella still attached to one arm, and pulled them out. This had later become another of Mum's many "tales of a common humanity" that we rolled our eyes over—how people were so good that even though poor, busy, uneducated, destitute, Hindu, Muslim, or Sikh, they had rushed to help her and fretted over her and escorted her home like a *rani*.

On those rainiest of days, some servants never made it to work in our house or any house. The slums in which they lived, and from where armies of them emerged to work in households all over Bombay every morning, became veritable high seas, cruelly washing away the paltry things that made up their lives. Savitribai, who had been with us for decades, would tell us the next day how the water entered every cooking vessel, clothing, and shoe they had in the hut and even the expensive things—their stove, a table, and a radio on which her children would listen to Hindi film songs. "*Memsaab*, today I am wearing wet sari only. Outside we are cooking on a big rock, but everywhere else there is only water. Everything is *khalaas*, *satyanas*. 'Completely finished.'" I remember her story creating a sick guilt over the pleasure I had had at my delicious day, but then casting it aside for the moment, as we always did, we Bombayites who had learned to live our lives amidst the unfathomable unfairness of it all, taking the desperate and hungry, glamorous and moneyed all in stride.

In the new Mumbai, some things are better and some are worse. The rich are immensely richer, the middle class are poorer or richer, and the poor are still desperate, but some, like my parents' maid Sunita, have dreams that are slowly, so slowly, being realized. Her only son, Viju, on whom she lavishes all her hopes and all her earnings from three different house-cleaning jobs, finished his schooling at the English-medium Sacred Heart Convent (the school attended by some of my neighborhood wall gang and cousins), is now in college, and who recently, sitting on my parents' sofa, spoke with a soft intensity of how he had to take care of his Mum because, "See, aunty, she has no one else. So I'm going to finish college and get a good job." I think the confident and intelligent Viju will make it in the new Mumbai, in the brave new India where some of the old social fault lines have finally been erased even while others have deepened.

If our birthday was on a Sunday, we would go for our inevitable Sunday family drive before going out for dinner. On some Sundays, we would go to Bandra Bandstand, walking by the sea, a gusty wind, unusual for Bombay, tossing our hair. "*Wah, wah*," Mum would say approvingly, "lovely strong wind today!" Mum and Paps would point out landmarks: the Sorabji Byramji Parsi sanatorium, an old grey stone building of forbiddingly Gothic exterior where old Parsis came to convalesce from smaller cities and towns and stared into the sea, and charities run by the Tatas or Godrejs or some other philanthropist family defrayed the bills, but yet their faces belied worry and disquiet; or the big white bungalow Villa Vienna that belonged to the Chemould art gallery-owning Gandhy family (who Paps admired for their pioneering work in the Bombay art scene), bought and transformed (later, after I had left Bombay) by actor Shah Rukh Khan—but at least he has left much of it intact, choosing to build behind the simple two-story colonial façade rather than destroy it.

Other Sunday evenings would commence after tea as Paps issued the dreaded summons, "*Chalo, chalo*, come on, where shall we go today?" And we would drive to Juhu beach, still accessible then, with some still-free space to walk on the dirty sands covered with driftwood, debris, and plastic bags and take in the balmy, fishy sea air. At Sea Face Hotel, the small shack of a "hotel" made up for its lacking with its unbeatable beach view. Sea Face Hotel's coconut-frond-covered balcony behind a wall right on the sandy shore was where we would sit and order hot and greasy potato chips, soft white triangular chicken sandwiches, and small crisp mutton samosas, orange Fanta, and coffee, and make perfunctory conversation. I often wonder if kids today still have to go for Sunday evening drives with their families, or has the new Mumbai emboldened them, freed them, unharnessed them from this weekly familial obligation? In the seventies, hippies from America and Europe still came in substantial numbers to Bombay, and a cheap hole like Sea Face Hotel would suit their budget. Rashna and I would watch covertly, admiring, puzzled, and repulsed—all at the same time—at the kind of confidence and freedom it would take to break free from the ties of city, family, uncles, aunties, friends to go off on your own, sit on a far-away beach and drink beer by yourself, as beggars on the beach outside taunted and entreated, and hawkers called. Surrounded by Indians with squalling kids and extended families in tow, these foreigners seemed to come from other worlds, worlds that intrigued and beckoned, but which I now know can be filled with great loneliness and emptiness of soul without the relentless embrace of family and friends that we took for granted.

The haunting beauty of these Bandra buildings or the disquiet brought in the wake of the forlorn, bedraggled hippies echoed the melancholy of another dying Sunday (unless, of course, it was a birthday Sunday, and we had our dinner to look forward to), and we would be lost in our thoughts; Paps immersed in his buildings and the permits and licenses that they would need and how he would avoid the gut-wrenching circle of bureaucratic bribes given and taken; Mum dwelling on her classes at Maneckji Cooper School (this was in the pre-preschool-at-our-home days), where she then taught high-school geography; and I feeling the familiar dread of the beginning of a new school week, where I knew the pace would be furiously set anew and there would be friends who would want to test allegiances and boys whom I wanted not to think about and other pressures that both invited and repelled. At home, we would all be relieved to see Mary banging around in the kitchen as usual, the note of normalcy helping to dispel the clouds and restore our equilibrium.

Our Bombay birthdays were merely quintessential Bombay days, heightened and enlarged because of a celebration, no matter how modest. Above all, they were a day in our city, spent in familiar, anticipated, or longed for locales that sharpened our attachment to Bombay and remained studded in our memories long after the party, so to speak, was over.

Chapter 12

THE DAY INDIRA WAS SHOT

Somehow, in my silly school-girl imaginings, my grandma, Coomie, whose visage was fast fading in my mind, became twinned with the powerful, mesmerizing image of Indira Gandhi with her flashing eyes, supercilious nose, and bold white stripe running through a perfectly waved coiffure. All the quiet strength and statuesque elegance that I remembered in Mamina, I thought I saw in Indira. As my love of the law was honed through Homi Uncle's staccato dictations, greedily inhaling the constitutional provisions—Fundamental rights, Directive principles—at school in Civics (easily my favorite subject), and obsessively reading the three newspapers that daily came to our house, I avidly followed the trajectory of her career. Indian politics was dominated through my life in the country by the larger-than-life figure and machinations of Indira.

Somewhere, though I would never have admitted it, so used was I to denying my own Parsi exceptionalism, there seemed another bond; by an unlikely turn of fate, Indira Nehru had married Feroze Gandhi, one of us, *aapro Parsi.* By most accounts, he was amiable enough, but hardly that exciting or accomplished, and certainly far from outstanding. However, their liaison still held the whiff of an eminently believable romance. A young girl from the most prominent of political families, an ordinary middle-class Parsi boy, meeting and falling in love in London in the 1930s, a city which must have seemed to both at once familiar and foreign. It was in England, of course, that Indira's father Jawaharlal Nehru had studied and been enthralled by Fabianism, poetry, and philosophy, and Indira had developed a sophistication much beyond her years that allowed her to proceed with confidence and hauteur in any circle, as Richard Nixon would one day find out. Feroze probably found comforting aspects of his middle-class upbringing sprinkled around him in London, in the shops and carriages, the last vestiges of servant-filled English life echoing the old order of 1930s and '40s Bombay.

The Day Indira Was Shot

Even before this connection, Nehru's Congress party had become the natural home for many of India's Parsis. Although his socialist leanings were pooh-poohed by an entrepreneurial community who had, for hundreds of years, built everything from arriving in India with nothing, the overtly secular complexion of the party and the progressive ideas embodied by the Nehru family made Parsis and other religious minorities the party's natural base at the time. Of course, much would change later: the Congress party would anger and estrange many erstwhile supporters, including of course Parsis, and Indira would commit acts that would threaten the core of India's democracy. But when Indira married Feroze, for a time, our Parsi connection was complete, and many a pearl-clad aunty admired the young mother and then widow, raising two sweet, round-faced little part-Parsi boys, Rajiv and Sanjay. Of course, politics and tradition would dictate that the boys would be raised Hindu, but these small facts did not dampen Parsi enthusiasm about the Nehru-Gandhi family. They talked like us, lived like us, and they even looked like us, *tadan Parsi*. In fact, in a curious coincidence (or perhaps at some point deliberately introduced in admiring mimicry?), the diminutive for our father, Paps, which we shared with Kayzad's family, was short for Papu, the appellation by which Indira had always referred to her father, Jawaharlal Nehru. Papu was not to be mistaken with Bapu, which was what the young Indira had referred to Mahatma Gandhi by. We imagined the young Indira running after her Papu and then tried to picture her calling him Paps and failed, feeling it unlikely that she would engage in such frivolity as creating a fanciful short-form.

During the decade of Indira's initial rule from 1966-1977, the country became mesmerized, pivoting around her great strengths and powerful weaknesses. As Bangladesh was liberated by the war of 1971, I have a vague memory of "black-outs"—Mum and Paps directing the servants to cover our windows with thick black paper so that West Breeze-Sea Breeze would not become targets of Pakistani aerial attacks. Although this was unlikely in a city as far south from the conflict as Bombay, air raid signals regularly wailed and people turned off lights at night when they got the sign. As it turned out, they need not have worried because the war lasted only a few weeks, and Pakistani jets never made it anywhere near Bombay. Indira had quickly won the war with decisiveness and brilliance, and also with the assistance of a newly-strengthened armed forces under the command of Field Marshal Sam Maneckshaw, India's first Field Marshal, improbably Parsi, although there were still quite a few Parsis left in the armed forces of independent India then. I later interviewed Maneckshaw for my dissertation on the India-Pakistan conflict, phoning him in his home in the hills in Ooty, where I recall he made points that added to the data I was collecting that would allow me to theorize about the role of communications in the India-Pakistan conflict, whether, if adequate official contact had been made and shared, things might have turned out differently. My dissertation did, in fact, conclude that in those conflicts where India and Pakistan had been proactive in communicating at the highest levels, there had been settlement without a full-blown war, whereas in others, as in 1971, when communications had broken down, war had ensued. When I had shared these dissertation ideas and theories with my mother, she had professed astonishment that I would be interested in wars and conflicts that had ended decades ago, and had encouraged a more modern subject. "All that is so long ago, *baebee*, nobody cares about it now. Stop wasting time on the past. And now that you're in America, why do you want to write about some forgotten India-Pakistan war anyway?" Gool was nothing if not direct and unsparing. But the more she was intent on embracing an updated present, the more I seemed to turn longingly to a time bygone.

Gandhi's own political and personal insecurities, a rowdy and robust opposition that was increasing its challenge to her rule, and infamous imperiousness (she was, after all, Indira!) came to a head as she declared an Emergency in 1975, suppressing, as allowed by the constitution, individual rights and civil liberties, and suspending elections indefinitely. However, the Emergency ultimately lasted only two years, during which innumerable opposition leaders were summarily imprisoned and citizens jailed without due process for crimes ranging from anti-state activity to petty smuggling. Indira surprisingly called elections in 1977, elections in which she and the Congress party were defeated for the first time, and soundly so, and India's democracy came of age.

I remember clearly two things from this Emergency period. The first is Paps urgently shushing Mum as she loudly declaimed and derided Indira in public on one occasion, *"Gheli thai gayeech?* Have you gone mad? They are putting people in jail left, right, and center these days for saying anything!" Mummy had immediately and uncharacteristically subsided. The second is the story told by Sunil, one of the occasionals in our wall gang. His uncle had been arrested under the Prevention of Smuggling Activities (COFEPOSA) Act. "Uncle has cancer," Sunil was talking rapidly so that the tears wouldn't come. "My mother is saying he may die in the jail. They have put him in one room with ten other prisoners and no toilet, nothing." The boys looked away, embarrassed, and my heart, never very sturdy, broke a little for this boy I didn't really know that well.

Small-time smuggling of washing machines, TVs, and fridges was de rigeur in those days, and many a housewife with the means to travel abroad (Singapore and Hong Kong were destinations of choice for these kinds of trips) would return with one coveted appliance to sell to buyers, eager for a choice of brands, to make a profit in rupees to cover both her trip and her shopping. To think of someone being brutally jailed under the COFEPOSA Act for this sort of thing, which my Mum would never have undertaken but would have strongly defended as justified anyway because of the poor quality of Indian appliances, was unthinkable, but many stories like this and many much, much worse—of murder, arbitrary arrest, and a fast-spreading story of forced vasectomies among the poor under the direction of Sanjay—made the rounds.

When the Emergency was lifted and elections were called in 1977, many believed that it was because Indira, in her deluded megalomania, believed that she was still loved, still India's "mother," and would surely win as she had always done. But I like to believe that she called elections even though she didn't have to, having assumed complete political powers in her hands by then, because of something deep within her that was of her father's and her grandfather's—a love of country, a respect for the political process, a knowledge that democracy, India's democracy, couldn't and shouldn't be so easily suspended, trifled with, and overturned.

Since that time, many of the excesses of the period have come to light, and political observers have been scathing about Gandhi, "madam," as they've derisively labeled her. What she did was indeed astonishing in its ugliness. It was the first and last time anyone took the fate of this difficult country and toyed with its constitution in this way for personal preference, and because they could. But I think also of the reasons that made her reverse herself, of giving up the complete power which she had wrongfully acquired, to allow Indians to cast their votes again. Unwittingly, she made Indian democracy grow up. Indians became surer of their singular achievement, their sustained consolidation of a rowdy and rambunctious and difficult democracy, a feat that only a handful of former colonies successfully achieved in the last century.

So my affair with Indira continued. Ironically, Paps, the aesthete, was greatly interested in politics, while Mum, the would-be writer and lover of literature, never showed much interest, often denouncing all politicians as crooks and thieves. Sitting with Paps on our West Breeze first floor balcony facing the garden, where green parrots once perched, and beyond which Sangeeta building's unchanging façade and my friends loomed, I would discuss the country's political life over scattered newspapers—*The Times of India* (at that time accused of being a "government" paper), *Indian Express,* the *Hindu* (both viewed as more independent), and assorted mid-afternoon dailies. The Congress's failings, the Janata party's prospects once it took over, official corruption that took our breath away, Indira's ignominious exit from Prime Minister to opposition leader, her own brief jailing, Sanjay's unspeakable forced sterilization program—I think Paps was shaken. In the shocking turmoil wrought by the Emergency, he had lived through what had been many Parsis' unspoken nightmare-fear since independence—that an unstable India, after the British left, would crush and obliterate a minority that constituted point infinitesimal of India's population and was protected precisely because of India's secular democratic tradition. This unease was despite the fact that Parsis were on the forefront of the independence movement, with leaders like Dadabhai Naoroji, Bhikhaji Cama, and Pherozeshah Mehta helping give political shape to the new India. In the decades since independence, as India's democracy has weathered greater challenges and matured, this fear has receded both in our community and in India in general. One doesn't hear the articulation of the "what if" scenarios that one used to, at least in reference to the demise of democratic politics. I think the community understands independence has come and gone, and the Congress era has come and gone, and the Parsis have survived still in the country that first gave them shelter a thousand years ago. Most Parsis believe the real threat in the new millennium is our demographic decline, and that far from the Indian government aiding in this, it is launching schemes, albeit ineffective (but that is not the government's fault), like Jiyo Parsi (Live, Parsis!) to encourage birth rates in the vanishing community.

With Paps by my side, I also saw Indira's spectacular comeback in a landslide election in 1980. By then, cynicism about the opposition Janata party was rife. In hindsight, I think Indians might have been kinder to the first change of party that had occurred since independence. Of course, it looked like the Janata politicians didn't know what they were doing, and they were hopelessly divided and not politically astute and made many, many rookie mistakes. It didn't help matters that none of them had the political background, sophistication, and regal, unruffled air and charismatic command of Indira. But they had formed a party and won elections against the old Congress (by 1978 the Congress-I, I for Indira) for the first time, establishing the path for an orderly change of power in the years to come, empowering poor and rich to vote with seriousness, effecting a path out of one-party rule; in the end a spectacular gift for India's political future.

In the ensuing years, I transitioned from Bombay Scottish to St. Xavier's College, that coveted place of my minor dreams, my mean-time dreams, while I waited to go to America. I had set my sights on St. Xavier's, Bombay's premier college and alma mater to those who intuitively and implicitly understood and loved Bombay (and the world) in the ways that I did, whose famed quadrangle framed by imposing, grey Gothic stone walls and arches had allowed and nurtured for hundreds of years the fragile dreams and yearnings for freedom of Bombay girls and boys. St. Xavier's, whose padres would become cherished teachers, setting an example through their own lives by leaving their own loves and comforts in distant Indian cities and countries like Spain to follow their calling in a far-away country that would become their very own. That this, like Bombay Scottish, had also been Mum's alma mater, I brushed off as a small annoyance. As I battled her through those teenage years, my motto seemed to have become to never cede to my mother any semblance of victory on any level.

At St. Xavier's, I was introduced to a world larger than Bombay Scottish's. Some of Bombay's best had gained inspiration here: cricketer Sunil Gavaskar; film-maker Ismail Merchant; conductor Zubin Mehta; cartoonist Mario Miranda; Supreme Court justice Soli Sorabjee; eminent constitutional scholar and economist Nani Palkhivala, who I later interviewed at Bombay House and whose signed copy of *We the People* still lives in my West Breeze bookcase, whose legendary kindness and graciousness accommodated a young graduate student with every seriousness. With millions of other Indians, Paps and I eagerly awaited Palkhivala's annual speeches at the Brabourne Stadium after the annual Budget was released. His analysis of the Budget was hailed for effortlessly cutting through the complexity of the numbers and the allocations to the various programs, ministries, and bureaucracies, and bringing clarity and understanding to laypersons. So, undoubtedly India's brightest had gained admission to St. Xavier's, although it must be conceded that many others certainly lacked much intellectual ambition and were there to be a part of what was unarguably the hippest (heppest, as we would say) crowd and the swellest social circle in Bombay with would-be models rubbing shoulders with budding actors like Salman Khan, whom I saw most often in the quadrangle before he became a mega star, striking poses and checking his hair.

In the 1980s, a reasonably high first class was enough to secure a place in the arts stream. When I got the marks to get in, Mum had announced proudly to Nilufer Aunty and countless others, "My Tinaz can do anything she sets her eyes on!" For this unswerving confidence in me and for so many incalculable gifts of strength and certitude, I never gave my mother any credit until I left India and discovered within myself, with some surprise, a core of steel, a part of me that was undeniably Gool's. Nilufer Aunty, of course, was unimpressed, as Kayzad had by then got into Grant Medical to start his medical training, even at that time no mean feat of the highest of marks. Today, I understand that it is next to impossible to get into any of these places unless you get near-perfect marks in every subject, a suspect development on so many levels, laughable and sad at the same time. Many of India's brightest now are routinely turned down by the likes of St. Xavier's and India's medical colleges and institutes of technology, its IITs, only to get full scholarships to Harvard and MIT. So many brilliant students, so little space and infrastructure, so little planning for future generations' needs. In America, these students blossom and return home these days to the new India to become, along with those students who opt to stay in India (and this includes socio-economic classes that could never have hoped to gain access to college even two decades ago), the new Indians who may finally make the hard and necessary changes. I am convinced one of these will be Viju, Sunita's son.

In those days, St. Xavier's had its fair share of slackers, especially in the Arts and Social Science streams. They filled the famed canteen to eat cheap samosas, admire themselves, and socialize, and bunked classes to attend movies at the nearby Metro cinema or go shopping at Colaba Causeway or Fashion Street across from Bombay Gymkhana, where if one looked hard enough, one could snag at dirt-cheap prices, incredible pieces of the latest fashions no doubt made in an Indian sweatshop somewhere and rejected for some minor flaw by the international fashion houses who had commissioned them. Or they otherwise enriched campus life outside of the classroom, ogling girls, approaching boys, giggling, fidgeting, laughing, searching. Others used the cultural canvas afforded us outside the gates of Xavier's: Jehangir Art Gallery, Max Mueller Bhavan and classes in Kala Ghoda on music appreciation by the brilliant pianist Fara Rustam, Bombay's most high-profile transgender who wore beautiful flowing silks and played with her long black hair as if still in disbelieving wonder, and kept us enraptured at the love story of Robert and Clara Schumann.

Within the college's old stone walls which trapped heavy, sultry air between the high wooden ceilings and fading but still vivid mosaic tiled floors, many subjects were taught in the grim, rote-focused way that school had emphasized, and I continued to chafe and continued to dream of America. But some moments were unexpectedly engaging. Fr. John Macia, jovial, twinkle-eyed behind his thick glasses, journeying from his homeland of Spain at an early age and living out the rest of his life here with only the slightest of Indian-Spanish accents to belie his roots, introduced us with passion and verve to Anthropology, to the life of the Todas and Nagas in the east Indian states, to social science methods of inquiry and ways of data collection to gain access to our subjects and their lives. Here we first learnt critical approaches to gaining knowledge that made us more aware of the class and ethnic biases that we unconsciously brought to our work as our starting point. This padre enraptured students in the class with his compassion, wit, guffawing humor, and big intellect and is still admiringly remembered by Xavierites of a certain age wherever they may be.

When I applied to American universities, Fr. Macia wrote me a recommendation that was as sparkling as he had been. I kept a copy of it for years, typed laboriously on Xavier's letterhead in the smudgy, black ink

The Day Indira Was Shot

that Indian typewriters favored, proof of my worth as I embarked on a new life in a new country much in the same fashion as he had done so many years ago, propelled by some of the same things: for me not a journey to serve God, of course, but the same great hunger for learning in big, broad, and soaring ways, and for the freedom to explore the world.

So it was that I was in St. Xavier's in 1984 when, during the morning hours, we got the shocking, unbelievable news—Indira had been shot. Because by then, disillusioned Indian commentary had become rife with fatalistic scenarios of Indian politics crumbling into chaos without Indira and the Congress; "no other alternative," they whined apathetically, "just look at what the Janata party did." Conflicting rumors immediately swirled through the college: she had been shot by her bodyguards, she was dead, she was not dead, she had survived, bullets couldn't kill her. Outside the grey stone walls, a chilling hush had descended on a usually honking, screeching, teeming, toiling city. Just to the left of the college, the busy intersection outside Metro Cinema that was usually choked with traffic was empty. People's faces belied grave anxiety. As news spread of rioting and retaliation, shops rapidly downed shutters in anticipation of common-for-such-times stone-throwing (Against what? Against whom?), the trains and BEST buses stopped working (Why? Why target trains because a leader had been assassinated?), and confusion reigned. I panicked a little as it became clear it was not necessarily safe to attempt to go back home to Santacruz, and indeed, there was no easy way to get back without the trains, but then I thought of the one place, close-by, familiar, and dear, where I went faithfully every week to talk and laugh with happiness, to Silloo Aunty's nephew-in-law, her most-loved boy, James Joyce to my Beckett, Chris Hitchens to my Ian McEwan, my own "brilliant friend," Firdaus.

Firdaus, small and fragile in his wheelchair, thin frail legs swinging uselessly, but oh so large in his presence! Loud, high-pitched cackle (later he told me, not without some pride, that it was yet another manifestation of his brittle bone disease, osteogenesis imperfecta), vast stores of knowledge, most widely read person that I knew, e.e. cummings-quoting, Iris Murdoch-admiring, Soviet-loathing, James Baldwin-loving, editorial-writing Firdaus, who had been so liberated by the unexpected and awful fate of spending life in a wheelchair that he proclaimed what he wanted, laughed as loudly as he could, read voraciously, lived large, observed keenly, and spared no one. By a happy chance of fate, Silloo's lovely boy was brought to Sea Breeze to spend every weekend of his life with her and Jam, and thence grew our friendship that became my secret delight, my comforting knowledge through years of tedious inward, growing-up turmoil and searching and intellectual ferment. Firdaus was the only one who knew more about the world of books, art, music, and politics than I did, and for that I was eternally grateful, although, of course, I never ceded this ground to him out loud.

Firdaus was outrageous, courageous, flamboyant, outspoken, and as sharp as a shining, thinly balanced razor blade. Many a weekend evening we spent on the wide, ground-floor steps of Sea Breeze, overlooking Silloo's garden with its overgrown copse of lemon trees and coconut palms. We argued, challenged, and deliciously discussed a recent book or essay, never concerned, as we must, incredibly, now be in Bombay, of mosquitoes or malaria or the degenerating chaos outside. We continued conversations on the lawns of Cusrow Baug, where he lived in the most premier of the Bombay Parsi colonies. Many such baugs (gardens), or housing colonies, exist all over north and south Bombay. They were built by Parsi philanthropic trusts like the Wadias, Godrejes, and Tatas to house Parsis in modest flats set among gathering spaces and open lawns. Consequently, some of them took the names of their benefactors, like Wadia Baug, or the Tata Blocks in Bandra, or Kharegat Colony on Hughes Road before the left turn in to my Mamina's house.

Cusrow Baug was located in prime Colaba real estate on the Colaba Causeway, minutes from the Taj and the Gateway. Today, the Causeway is a shabbier self, quite past its peak of glittering shops and cutting-edge footwear and clothing stores, and unsure of what it really is any more. Here my grandmother had her favorite Chinese-owned shoe shops that custom-made exquisite and durable shoes, and my mother had ordered her delicate white pointed-toe wedding shoes from one of these long gone Chinese stores. Fashion and glitter, the Causeway has ceded to the shopping-savvy Bandra, Linking Road, and other locales now known for their innovative design. But it has retained its exotic air, the mixture of old-world-new-world, European, Arab, hippy, Indian mingling; and daring and *bhindaas*, free, unfettered cafés, smoky bars, and antique shops, which invite tourists misguidedly seeking, like the Australian hippy-criminal-turned author "Shantaram," some hidden knowledge of the "real" Bombay, which Colaba may or may not possess. One such bohemian café, Leopold, our occasional hang-out from St. Xavier's, invited the terrorists' wrath on November 26, 2011 for just such an air of freedom and laissez-faire; the fanatics sought to shoot at the heart of Bombay's tolerance and moderation. In those days, though, Firdaus loudly proclaimed that he could never live south of Colaba ("never So-Co, darling"), that life in Santacruz was provincial and unthinkable. I, of course, robustly and laughingly defended my beloved suburb, but a part of me silently agreed, singing to the tune of magical South Bombay with all its seeming possibilities.

So it was to Cusrow Baug that I turned on that chilling morning, not knowing, even as four of us Xavierites managed to finally get one of only a few taxis available for sharing, whether Indira really had been killed. All India Radio had not made an official pronouncement yet, and the normally thronging roads were eerily quiet. To this the taxi driver added his own confused take on the situation. It was at times like this—rare, but real—that I was unsure of my country: unsure if a mob could descend from nowhere to overturn our vehicle, unsure if someone would throw a flame or start a march, a *morcha* that might turn into a violent frenzy, unsure if I, with my olive skin, distinct looks, and strange religion, would become the target of an incensed attack. But on that day we saw no violence. No *morchas* had started yet, no sloganeering, just an uneasy quietude, a paucity of people and vehicles; on the face of it, Bombay as it might have been forty years ago when Gool would have held court at St. Xavier's.

I held my breath until I was dropped off at the gates of Cusrow Baug, all of us watchful, saying little. I walked through the vast wood-and-iron entrance gates, which I had never seen closed and which were that day wide open as usual, and entered the walled community, unimaginative blocks of flats with red-tiled roofs set in long rows along orderly streets. These were refreshed by green lawns, gardens, and the distinct lack of any garbage or dirt one would see routinely on any Bombay road. I thought again, as I always did when I went to Cusrow Baug, of the Jews decades ago living in just such communities, thinking that numbers meant strength and safety, only to find themselves extinguished in their homes and among their own when the Nazis descended.

No one had sought to exterminate the Parsis, of course; in fact, India had provided support and affection, and for this Parsis were always grateful. But I think this unspoken fear was surely one that every Parsi carried around but laughingly dismissed in public. "*Arre*, no one will touch us, it would be too easy, *yaar*. *Bus*, in five minutes we would all be finished if they tried!" But later, after I left India, Mum and Dad told me that such a nightmare had indeed become reality in Bombay, not for Parsis, but for some of Bombay's Muslims. When the Hindu-Muslim riots broke in Bombay in 1992, the first fierce communal rioting of its kind in the city since independence, erupting because of the conflict over the Babri Masjid in Ayodhya, Mum and Dad's Muslim neighbors, tenants who were temporarily living in Kashmira Aunty's ground-floor flat in West Breeze, had run upstairs, fearful, and asked if they might flee up the internal wooden staircase built by my grandfather to our flat and Amy Aunty's above "if the need arose."

"What did you say?" I held my breath.

"Of course, *baebee*, we said yes, what else?"

The need had not arisen, but the family left the ground-floor flat with its wide glass doors opening into the front garden and the bougainvillea and coconut trees soon afterward, investing in a flat on a higher floor nearby in Bandra. I heard that some Muslims, even in high-rises, were not as safe. But I also heard that in other buildings, Hindu neighbors made sure that every identifying name-plate beside each building flat number was removed, just in case.

I walked faster, past the fire-temple, the Agiary with its wide entrance adorned with *godhas* and *farohars*, the winged angels and half-bulls from our Persian past that we liked to wear around our necks and display on our buildings and even make stickers of to place on our cars. Rounding the last stretch of street, I saw Thrity Aunty hanging out of the flat window, white curls bobbing, waving me up with the usual crazy sweeps of her arms. All around was simply peace and order, cars parked in straight lines, hedges manicured, a perfectly sunny and calm morning in Cusrow Baug. As I ran up the steps to the first floor, Firdaus was somber, too upset to assume the various faux-historical postures he usually greeted me with: Winston Churchill squinting his eyes against the fake smoke of his elegantly held imaginary cigar; Marlene Dietrich in mid-song, one thin bony shoulder thrusting out of the wheel-chair; Marilyn Monroe batting long black lashes (we all agreed his own mile-long lashes framing sparkling black eyes were wasted on a boy). BBC world service radio, turned up to deafening levels, confirmed that Indira was dead.

In the next two days I spoke shakily to Mum and Dad, and each time they urged me to wait another day. News of retribution against the Sikhs, riots in Delhi that targeted the community for the sins of Gandhi's bodyguards, spread all over the country. Khushwant Singh, writer, provocateur, and India's most famous Sardar, lashed out bitterly against the Congress for colluding in the carnage. But in Bombay, we had never let communal passions get the better of us, not even during independence. And so, in 1984 they didn't, until things changed irrevocably after 1992. In that year, the four hundred year old Babri Masjid in Ayodhya was overrun and destroyed by Hindu zealots, and riots between Hindus and Muslims broke out across the country, including in Bombay, with thousands losing their lives. Acts of domestic terrorism by Muslim fanatics accelerated in the next decades, creating vicious cycles of terrorism and retaliation as relations between the two communities deteriorated to their worst levels since independence.

In my Bombay, we were still some years away from that. We knew that we were all different, and we had learnt how to live with each other. In retrospect, I wonder how we *unlearnt* this toleration. Or perhaps under the surface, tensions unknown to Parsis had always lurked and then they had boiled over. But in 1984, we felt protective of the Sikhs, made prominent by their *pagris*, the initial target of the country's shock and outrage. Firdaus, Thrity Aunty, Hushedar Uncle, and I watched Doordarshan for

The Day Indira Was Shot

updates as mournful Indian classical music played and stills of an Indira, larger-than-even-life in death, filled the screen. Later, the funeral was televised live, one of the first live television "events" that we ever saw on TV, the Gandhis, Sonia, Rajiv, and the children reunited momentarily at the smoke-hazed funeral pyre with Maneka and Varun. The latter two, mother and son, were all that remained of the other much-loved son, Sanjay, deceased before his doting mother in an airplane crash. Rajiv, the reluctant politician, realized through the wafting smoke that his day on the political stage had unceremoniously arrived. The Italian-born Sonia's greatest fear, for her husband's future safety, jockeyed with her real grief for the mother-in-law who had become a mother in a country that had become hers as it had become Uschi Aunty's decades before her.

During those three days, we remained in Cusrow Baug in a cocoon woven by the sturdy yellow-brown walls of the compound. Within the walls, life seemed to continue as normal, cars robustly revving up, daily vendors—*dudhwala, paowalla, bhajiwalla, paperwalla*—selling their wares, doddering oldies in pearls and scarves gathering at the lawns of the modest in-house Cusrow Baug Club across from Firdaus's flat to play cards and carom, and down oily samosas and whisky. At some point, I put Indira out of my mind and gave in to the sheer delicious enjoyment of the unplanned Cusrow Baug stay with Firdaus's clever friends and his books and music, and Thrity Aunty's gay and voluble presence that might have masked her unuttered sadness. We took late-night walks through the baug, wheeling Firdaus's chair and feeling triumphant because surely no one else in the whole colony could understand the depths of our discussions. We were exhilarated at being us, and demolished all others with delight: Dharmendra, the hapless bachelor in flat 20 C, mockingly so nicknamed for his full film-star mane of hair and hairy exposed chest; frail little Freny Aunty in flat 40 S who we had re-christened shuttupyaarfreny because we had once heard her nieces say exactly that to her before pushing her rudely into a waiting taxi; stern and ramrod straight octogenarian Tehmina Mistry, loudly berating a shrinking, smirking, pimply youth for leaving his cycle in the building doorway for her to trip over.

Then, on the third day, after conferring with Mum and Paps, I was told that it was fine to come home, to "just take a taxi all the way, *baebee*, no trains, and be careful, *jaan*." Stepping foot for the first time in three days outside the compound walls with its gates, as always, open to the causeway, I hailed a cab and started out. Life seemed normal; screeching traffic was back on the roads and crowds jostled as if the eerie day of Indira's assassination had never happened. In the middle of the causeway, before we turned left towards Firdaus's Campion School and then past the Oval Maidan and thence to the svelte stretch of Marine Drive where a decade ago I had walked in the sultry sea-breeze every Saturday evening with my Mamina, my eyes caught in shock and revulsion the sight of a single store-front. Modest and set between a larger shoe store (closed) and restaurant (filled with customers), it was burnt to the ground in a perfectly targeted act of revenge, a huge unblinking eye that looked reproachfully across towards Delhi Darbar, scene of so many illicitly-delicious *biryanis* eaten during college bunks. It had been a sari shop, owned for twenty years by a "cut" Sikh, a sardar who had not adopted (or rejected at some point) the turban and flowing beard specified by the Guru, but who to all others and for all intents and purposes evidently retained his identity as a Sikh in a country where one's immutable first identity is always one's ethnic group—what's your caste, what's your religion, what language do you speak at home? What are you? Sindhi? Punjabi? Parsi? Marwari? Sikh?

The political pundits in newspapers and on Doordarshan TV and a ruminating Paps had a field day with their "now what?" scenarios. Which political party would come to power? Was it the finish of secularism? Was it the end of Indian nationalism and the acceleration of hyphenated India, a reversion to our fragmented pre-British past? Was it the end of democracy itself, then barely four decades old? Would India stay together or fracture along ethnic and communal lines? And we, who had grown up with Indira and seen her through her triumphs and failures, felt a loss that we couldn't properly articulate. It would be too gauche to be sad or fearful, to wail in the streets like thousands of other Indians, the poor and disenfranchised who had felt championed by her and her poverty-alleviation (to critics, vote-maximizing) schemes and for whom she was mother, *mata*, not madam; but it would be permissible to be somber, to drop the cool for a bit and dwell on the sudden and unceremonious end of an era.

A few years later, I would leave India and soon after that, Indira's son Rajiv would take the first steps towards opening up the country's economy to foreign investment, setting up the acceleration under Congress Prime Minister P.V. Narasimha Rao, who took over when Rajiv himself was assassinated in 1991. He was blown up by a Tamil suicide bomber nursing grievances about India's role in the Sri Lankan conflict between Tamils and Sinhalese, and left behind a widow who had seen her worst fears finally realized in a most cruel déjà vu of smoke and funeral pyre, and two stolid children who would become the bedrock of her life and support. When I returned, the country was transforming itself into something else: the city, my Bombay, had become Mumbai, and Plato's belief in the permanence of change had been underscored again.

Chapter 13

LEAVING BOMBAY

I spent the last two years at St. Xavier's feverishly researching universities that would allow me to go to America, finally, once and for all, the America of my longing. Many classmates were involved in the same pursuit, and the U.S. Information Service at Marine Lines became very familiar to us as we attended confusing meetings where speakers walked us through the labyrinth of requirements that would need to be met before we could hope to leave and shared large envelopes filled with materials that arrived from universities and colleges. We studied for the GRE exam and sneered over the TOEFL—English as a foreign language indeed! English was as much an Indian language as any of the other hundred plus major ones, and for some Indians, it was their best language, the language they wrote in, argued in, and dreamt in. Primary in my mind was the realization that I could not go anywhere without a full scholarship. The privileged life of my childhood had turned into comfortable middle-classness for us in West Breeze, but this could not conceivably stretch to pay American fees. I was also determined that my parents should not have to lose their daughter to another country *and* have to pay for it.

The remaining hours were taken up by cursory studying for college exams, roaming around town with college mates, foreign films at Sterling Cinema where we thrilled to Catherine Deneuve and Truffaut and Bergman and pretended to understand Rainer Werner Fassbinder's plotless and stilted scenes (deep, *yaar*). Less intellectually inclined activities included *biryanis* at Delhi Darbar that we argued over and meticulously divided to stretch limited pocket money and long, crisp paper *dosas* with steaming coffees at Madras Café around the corner from Xavier's, where office workers and manual laborers and college girls and boys brushed shoulders with ease. At home in Bandra-Santacruz-Juhu, there were parties and discos to attend, the wall gang, late-night Carter Road drives in various decrepit and crawling vehicles, dressing up, high heels and going out.

At one such party, just when I was begging Neera, Reena, and other assorted girls I had gone with to leave, please, it was so boring, and had already, as I often did, switched my internal focus on to America, flip, just like that, I met the Engineer. A dour, surly, thin boy with startling, staring mud-green eyes, he showed such little reaction to anything that I immediately became interested. Later, he called. By then we had our own telephone line at West Breeze first floor, and I was spared the indignity of the first twelve years of my life, when phone calls from friends and would-be suitors alike were received upstairs at Amy Aunty's and a small bell was pulled from upstairs which rang vigorously in a window outside our flat below and caused us to rush upstairs breathlessly, two steps at a time to shamefacedly take our calls, imagining Amy censorious in the background. In reality she never once said anything, ever, and calmly and graciously handed over each and every call no matter how irritating it must have been for their family.

More than anything, I was enamored by who he was: engineering student, so smart he may even be my equal, (although I could teach him a thing or two about literature and music: Sylvia Plath, Doris Lessing, Iris Murdoch, Andre Brink, Alice Walker, Bach's mind-turning Goldberg Variations, these had become my constant diet and salvation), taciturn, watchful, maddening, not the average boring boy. He had glistening brown skin and deep brown-green eyes that never gave anything away. Always having held men at bay, preferring instead to carry on my relationships in my head with unattainable icons or unavailable boys, I found, to my surprise, that I didn't necessarily want to push this one away.

My last two years in Bombay I spent with the Engineer in tow, immersed in his world and impressed by his friends who were studying to be architects, pilots, and doctors. His very cool parents threw chic parties, complete with waiters who walked around with new-fangled appetizers like cocktail samosas, chicken lollipops, and baby-corn cakes, in their minimalist bungalow built in the sixties and so unlike the old familiar Parsi abodes and tabelas I was used to. In Bombay, all existing bungalows seemed to have been built before independence and certainly before the fifties, but his (like Raja-Rani's in our neighborhood lane between West Breeze and Sangeeta Building) was probably one of very few that was built in the era when tall building blocks started to become the norm in the space-starved city. The inside was all sleek minimalism and pop art and, because I was so enamored of all things to do with him, this quickly became my favorite style, trumping for a while my long love-affair with mid-century modernism and the architecture of the era of my father and his friends. We went to rock concerts and fledgling jazz bands, walked on the dirty sands of Juhu beach which was minutes from his house and going towards which we would pass the bungalow of Bollywood great Dharmendra (although it may have been someone else, Juhu was swimming with film-star types) who was their neighbor and apparent family friend (mildly interesting and something to casually drop at the dinner table in secretly-disguised triumph). We took with us Gopi, his lumbering brown Alsatian who had a reputation for a tricky temper but who was a lamb when we lounged around reading or listening to Coltrane or Spyrogyra or (my turn!) the Grieg piano concerto which he warned he could only take so much of. We ate at the hands of Maharaj, the ancient cook (Why such an exalted title? It turned out many Gujrati families gave this curious appellation to their cooks, and I suppose it was fitting since they were the kings of their kitchens!), who produced the most delectable and unfamiliar delicacies with no meat in sight. I could hear Gool's astonished voice in my head ("What, no *gos*, *baebee*?") as we demolished fat buttery *theplas* with methi and spinach, many-colored *dals* redolent with the Gujrati sweet-tangy-spicy flavors, *puris* we dipped in four different kinds of mango achars and chutneys after our walks before his parents could return from their medical practice for dinner, much to Maharaj's disgust.

So interested was I in the Engineer that I might have been tempted to chuck away all the plans for America: after all, didn't I have everything I could ever want right here in Bombay *and* the murky serious-mocking eyes that would tease only me forever? I think sometimes I was allured by this possibility, but at other times, I had the curious feeling of standing outside the room, the bungalow, even myself, and looking in at us, trying to bring the two together, image and reality, and, once again, failing.

One day, the Engineer asked me if I intended to come back to Bombay and I answered honestly that it was unlikely. He asked me if I would take with me a ring set with a simple stone that had belonged to his grandmother, and I answered that I could not. Then he asked what about him and what about us, and I answered who knew. But still my Engineer didn't abandon me, and still he sat in my room and helped me with the GRE Math and quizzed me on the GRE vocabulary, knowing all the while that the higher test scores would inevitably take me ever closer to America and ever further away from our Bombay life.

Out of the six universities I applied to, three offered me scholarships and two offered me full scholarships, the minimum goal I had set for myself to be able to go. I remember the first one, opened with shaking hands and sweating brow, and the slowly expelled breath: finally, it was here—the irrevocable proof that I would now go to America. Someone named Dr. Williams (whom I later wrote to and spelt out without holding back what his letter had meant; I hope the mild, reserved mid-westerner hadn't been too embarrassed) had invited me to join his department somewhere in Ohio, covering all the tuition and fees, everything, while also offering what seemed to be a magnificent stipend.

Mum and Paps, excited but calm, preoccupied with their work, lives, friends, and parties, unknowing then that this girl, this daughter, would finish her degree and begin another, and then begin a job and a life, and then never live in Bombay again; that another daughter, the one Mum had tried to pretend was a sports-loving boy as long as she could, and that they both thought they would still have with them, would also follow, and that the years would hurtle forward, friends would peel away and the parties would die out and Paps would close his practice and store away the blueprints and models and pens and give away the office in Flora Fountain that Rashna and I had loved to eat chicken sandwiches in. They couldn't have known that the two of them would grow old together and talk to their girls on Skype and fall in love with their grandkids (finally, the boys Gool never had!) and see them once a year instead of all the time, and that their girls would carry this burden, this guilt with them forever, haunted by the stooped backs and grayed hair and confused looks and utterly destroyed by the enormous generosity and love that propelled both parents to not once, never ever, utter these words to them: why didn't you come back?

On the last day, a veritable army made it known that they would be coming to see Tinaz off at the airport. From upstairs, Nader Uncle, who himself had always proudly proclaimed that he would never leave the shores of apru India, best in the world, Amy Aunty and Sorab; from passay next door Silloo-Jam and the cousins upstairs; from Gowalia Tank Homi Uncle and Kayzad; Mum, Paps and Rashna and of course the ever-faithful Roda Aunty and unbeknownst to all of them, the Engineer and his Juhu gang, the pilot-in-training friend having got them all special passes to proceed into the bowels of the airport, those being the days before terrorism-fuelled obsessive airport security. Filled with the worry of leaving with my life in two suitcases, I half wished that they would all have just stayed home!

At the airport, many breathless exhortations flew through the air. From Mum, a familiar one: "Don't take anything from strangers, *dikra*, remember, remember!" Mum had been somehow scarred from watching films like *Bangkok Hilton* and *Midnight Express* and always harbored a fear of her daughters being hauled away by cops and dogs for inadvertently carrying someone else's drugs. From Silloo, "Don't forget to write every month, over there aerogrammes are very cheap, very cheap. We'll be waiting to hear all the news, everything, everything, don't forget!" Nader Uncle, ponderously: "Do not forget your motherland, India! Best country in the world bar none! No country like India!" Earlier in Santacruz, Kobad Uncle had released a breathless volley of "goodbye, godbless, ta-ta, see you, bye-bye," as I had escaped down the old wood stairs, gripping the polished banisters hard, and turning to look up at him and Ketty framed in the old Sea Breeze doorway one more time.

For days, my heart had been breaking bit by bit, but now I just wanted to be done. I still had to deal with the Engineer, who at this moment was waiting at a designated spot on the lower level, permitted in by the secretly-secured passes. Waving madly at the relatives and swearing that I would write every week on the cheap-cheap aerogrammes and never forget India, and feeling horribly guilty but too busy and frazzled to feel too sad, I turned and ran downstairs as soon as they were all safely out of sight. There, at the café as we had arranged, waited the Engineer with his familiar scowl in place and the friends hanging loosely around, throwing bored punches at each other, casually swearing up and down, and smoking one cigarette after another (again, these were undoubtedly the days before both terrorism and environmental-awareness). As soon as I arrived, the friends dutifully scattered and the Engineer and I stood looking awkwardly at each other. I tried not to think of how little time I had left to go through immigration and thence on to the departure gate.

Somehow, we got through the long minutes, not having anything to say, I politely plucking away an errant arm on my shoulder that somehow seemed out of place in the busy purposeful airport. Finally, he said he would accompany me upstairs so that I could go on to immigration. He impatiently stabbed the elevator button, perhaps also feeling that this scene had played itself out, but who knew? He wasn't usually one to say what he felt.

Almost sighing with relief, I stepped in with him, now finally starting to feel the beginnings of enormous longing and loss, the leaving behind of a life. As the elevator pinged open on the upper floor, I saw to my horror the gaggle of extended Pavri-Rustoms were still milling around and at that moment looking directly at us in confusion and delight and starting to babble excitedly. I allowed the Engineer to slink away and shame-facedly made up some mangled excuse for why I was riding an elevator back up to the floor where I had left them, and where I was supposed to stay in the first place. The long goodbyes cranked up again, and all the old advice started another robust cycle—strangers, drugs, India, best, letters, remember, write, write!

For months afterwards, I hugged closely to myself the image of the cantankerous, loud, and achingly familiar group that I bade goodbye to, bumped into again, and waved farewell to one last time as a Bombay girl. For a while, I was horrified at how the door had opened onto my deception, and how my relatives and the forbidden boyfriend stared at each other in shock and disbelief. Then, the humor of the situation caught up with me and livened up my first year in Ohio every time I summoned up what Rashna and I would forever call in Hindi film fashion, "the parting scene."

So I left Bombay, but, as they say in that oldest of clichés, Bombay never left me. Just as all my waking dreams in Bombay were of America, so all my nightly dreams in America now became, unbidden, sometimes unwelcome, but always, of Bombay. Vivid, multi-colored dramas unfold many a night, of Roda Aunty, impromptu cricket at Palamkot Hall and Khalakdina Terrace, that dried up old twig Miss Pai handing out a Math test where every equation looks unfamiliar. I see Mathews again, with thin lips twitching, summoning up another hapless boy for a caning, and I argue with Firdaus on the wide, curving Sea Breeze veranda and never, never admit defeat. Dreams, sometimes, of classmates that I have long forgotten, the call of the *bhel-walla* of an evening, the wind on Marine Drive as I clutch my Mamina's hand, and once in a long while, of an unremembered and foolish school crush: this dream where I am trying to find him again, looking frantically for his number in our old tattered brown family phone diary in West Breeze only for the number to elude me and the diary go missing and then finally, on a torn chit of paper, finding it at last, actual numbers clearly written, and dialing it on the old black rotary phone, fingers clumsy with anticipation, and then…

Waking up in America.

Glossary

The majority of the words in this book are Gujrati, the Parsi-Gujrati dialect spoken by India's Parsis ever since their arrival on the shores of what is now Gujrat state (and what were then kingdoms), a thousand years ago. Others are Hindi, reflecting the easy use of multiple languages, sometimes in the same conversation, that is common in India.

Achar: spicy pickle of mango, lime, carrot, or other vegetables in limitless variations, universally eaten in India as a condiment.

Agiary: fire temple, place of worship of Zoroastrian Parsis where, by custom, entry is permitted only to members of the community.

Arre (ar-ray): "Oh, come on!"

Baksheesh: a gift of money; sometimes, a bribe of money.

Bania: small, family-owned corner grocery shop; there are innumerable of these shops at every corner in the city.

Bechari: poor thing.

Bhajan: religious song.

Bhakra: sweet, puffed Parsi doughnut.

Bheja: brains of goat.

Bhel: street food; a mélange of puffed rice, fried flour straws, chutneys, and condiments.

Bhindaas: carefree, bold.

Bhonu: food; lunch or dinner.

Bilkul: exactly like.

Bus: enough; finished; that's all; end of story.

Chai: tea.

Chalo: come; come on.

Channa: gram; chickpea. Often eaten in a curry or boiled and spiced from street vendors.

Chappals: slippers.

Chee chee: sound of disapproval.

Chooras: fried, spiced lentils and puffed rice that can accompany tea, drinks, etc.

Churails: banshees; ghosts.

Crore: 100,000 lakhs.

Dabba: box; tiffin-box.

Dal: spiced lentils of different kinds.

Dastur/dasturji: Parsi Zoroastrian priest; the ending in ji is a sign of respect, often added to Indian names of elders.

Dikra: dear.

Dosa: long, crisp savory crepe.

Dudhwala: milk seller. These sellers could sell their wares in handcarts on the road, in small roadside shops, or baskets and vessels, which they carried door to door.

Ekdam: exactly, absolutely, just like.

Farohar: Also called a fravashi; the winged bull, which in Zoroastrian mythology is said to represent a guardian angel. If there is one symbol that represents Parsi Zoroastrians, it is this.

Feta: a tall, glossy black hat worn for traditional Parsi Zoroastrian ceremonies.

Ganthia: thin sticks of flour or gram flour that are spiced and fried.

Garas: colorful, richly embroidered Parsi saris that were first brought from China centuries ago.

Ghats: hills, particularly the hills in Maharashtra state.

Godha: Zoroastrian/ancient Persian symbol of a bull.

Gos: mutton.

Gully/gullies: small lanes and by-lanes.

Gurkha: a watchman, gate-keeper; named after the famed gurkha tribes from north-east India and Nepal, who had proven themselves to be fierce warriors during World War II. Gurkha regiments still exist in the Nepali and Indian armies.

Jaan: dear.

Kadai: big, copper cooking pan.

Kamakli: foolish.

Khalaas: finished; over; done.

Khandaan/khandaani: family/ancestral.

Kusti: sacred thread worn around the waist of Parsi Zoroastrians after their *navjotes*.

Lakh: 100,000; approximately $1,600 dollars to 1 lakh rupees.

Lookahs: hangers-on; those without gainful work.

Maidan: large, open grounds or fields for meetings or sports.

Mali: gardener.

Mathoobanoo: traditional headscarf worn by conservative Parsi women, mainly in earlier times.

Matka: informal, illegal gambling game.

Morcha: demonstration, sometimes leading to violence.

Mori: traditional bathroom of stone; often, these were present in the corner of traditional kitchens to facilitate the washing of utensils.

Nariel pani: coconut water.

Navjote: the Zoroastrian coming of age ceremony, where each child must learn the main prayers from the holy book, the Zend Avesta, in the original language of Avesta.

Pagri: turban.

Pakora: spicy vegetable fritters.

Pallu/palla: the drape of the sari, which goes over one shoulder and finishes its fall.

Pao bhaji: a street food of spicy potato mixture scooped up with bread.

Paowalla: bread seller.

Pareekas: packets or envelopes filled with gift money, given at birthdays, *navjotes*, weddings.

Passay: next door.

Patrel: stuffed taro leaves; often a Parsi teatime snack.

Phoren: foreign; term also used sarcastically to acknowledge Indians' love of things that were from abroad, particularly during the socialist/mixed economy years when these things were very difficult for the average Indian to obtain, and were hence coveted even more.

Prasad: blessed sweets given at temples to worshippers.

Pulao: baked rice made with spices and herbs, chicken or mutton, and decorated with cashews, currents, and (particularly for Parsis) sliced boiled eggs and caramelized onions. Different Indian communities would prepare a *pulao* or *palao* or *pilau* with their own variation.

Punkha: a large fan, hand-held or electric.

Puri: fluffy fried flatbread.

Rani: queen.

Sabziwala: vegetable seller.

Sagan: a celebration. A sagan-ni-sais was a large, round, silver salver that held silver bottles for rosewater, trays for the garlands of flowers, and the silver urn for the red powder that would form the sagan-no-tillo, the ceremonial red mark on the forehead. These loaded salvers made their appearance at all *navotes* and weddings.

Sardar: a Sikh gentleman.

Satyanas: complete ruin.

Sudras: white muslin undershirts that Parsi Zoroastrians must wear under their clothes after their *navjotes*; both the *sudra* and *kusti* (an intricately woven sacred thread to be tied around the *sudra*) are together meant to protect one from life's ills.

Tabela: horse stables.

Tadan: exactly like; the copy of.

Talla: lock.

Tamasha: an avoidable or unavoidable drama or chaos.

Glossary

Tapelas: large, traditional vessels made of copper or aluminum, used for cooking large quantities of food.

Taza; taza-taza: fresh.

Thepla: thick flatbread, often baked with vegetables like methi (fenugreek), spinach, or herbs.

Tillo/tilla: ceremonial red mark on the forehead.

Topi: a cap or hat.

Vohu Man/Vohu Manah: in the Avestan language, the good mind. A moral imperative for Zoroastrians to always accomplish tasks at hand with integrity.

Wada pao: fried, spicy potato patty served in a small bun smeared with green chutney; often served in road-side stalls.

Wah, wah: an exclamation meaning wonderful or good job.

Yaar: dear.